The LIFE
AND PROMOTION OF AN
ABUSED
Woman

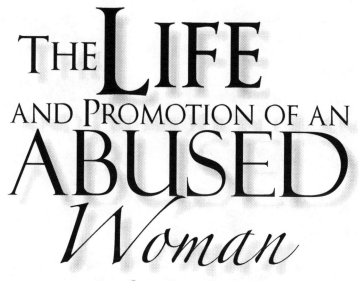

THE LIFE
AND PROMOTION OF AN
ABUSED
Woman

OVERCOMING OBSTACLES WITH PATIENCE

This document shows that, despite living in an abusive situation, you can survive the threats by focusing on the Lord Jesus, and connecting with Him in the Gospel. It explains that turning to drugs or alcohol is not an option. Even though the author is constantly being attacked by witchcraft, knowing Jesus Christ as a deliverer makes life worth living.

MARY JOHNSON, PH.D

To order additional copies of this book, contact:
Xlibris Corporation
1-888-795-4274
www.Xlibris.com
Orders@Xlibris.com
126067

Dedication

I dedicate this book to my Heavenly Father, the Father of our Lord and Savior Jesus Christ, who spared my life to write and tell of the things that are happening to thousands of women, and even men, in this era. I dedicate my life and this book completely to Him. At the completion of this work, the Lord gave me the title of the book.

A little Island in the Caribbean, Grenada, very mountainous, green and well nourished with the fallen, seasonal rain surrounded by water, you can feel the sea breeze as you move around the Island, the beeches with its white sand and the sea glittering from the sun; it is the land of spice where minerals are found in the natural soil, Dr. Mary Johnson was born on that soil, the Island of Grenada. She is a retired nurse, musician, author and missionary to the nation. Acquiring her nursing education in London, England, Mary migrated to America with her husband and two daughters. Despite an abusive marriage, she tried hard to maintain her integrity. It reached the point where the abuse became unbearable and, as a result, filed for divorce. Despite having four children, Mary had to run for her life. In 1972, the bitterly contested divorce became final. Given custody of the four children, she dare not take them, for their father was determined to have them reside with him. He said, angrily, "I'll kill them all." Mary kept her sanity by furthering her education, occupying herself in the nursing profession and engaging in missionary work.

In 1983, Mary began missionary work throughout the nations, beginning at her home town, Grenada and other Caribbean Islands such as Trinidad and Tobago, Saint Vincent and the Grenadines, Jamaica and Bolivia—South America. She travelled extensively, beginning with England, India, China, Philippines, Hong Kong, Asia, Israel and Rome, lastly Egypt and Israel.

Many years ago the Lord demands that Mary begins to write, supporting her work with scriptures. She authored her first book, "Branded for Missions" in 2005. Today, she writes about her life experiences, from childhood to her senior years. She hopes to encourage the readers to maintain their integrity despite the hard knocks that accompany life in general. You can cope with post-abusive marriage by engaging in activities that will motivate and empower you to move on and succeed in life. Mary used the occasion to better herself academically, socially and spiritually, with the help of God. She also shares her experience with anger and unforgiveness, a painful situation that affects thousands of individuals emotionally and spiritually. Mary experienced childhood abuse, attempted rape, and abusive marriage. She says, in an abusive marriage after a bitter, contested divorce, you have to be prepared for war, especially when young children are involved in the marriage.

TABLE OF CONTENTS

Introduction XI
1   A Childhood view 15

Chapters

2   Another get-away 20
3   Time for change 25
4   Yearly evaluation 30
5   Back home 36
6   Higher Education 42
7   Back on the job 49
8   A day in prison 54
9   Missionary endeavor 57
10 Your own backyard 65
11 Anger and unforgiveness 71
12 Obstacles part of the territory 78
13 Assigned to teach 86
14 On the battlefield 91
15 A child of divorced parents 96
16 Intercessors' call 101
17 Culture differentiation in marriage 108
18 God is full of surprises 115
19 Excitement in the air 120
20 Destination beyond the norm 126
21 Conflict management 135
22 Prayer changes things 143
23 Summary 153
24 Epilogue 157

INTRODUCTION

When your life appears to be in shambles and all hope seems to be lost, you need not give up. Too often individuals throw in the towel just as God is getting ready to show up in their lives and in their situations. Are you in an abusive marriage and are afraid for your life? As an individual I experienced harsh punishment as a child. Growing up in Grenada, insisting on having my choice of foods, I moved from one family to another. Attempted rape twice as a child, I began traveling at the age of fourteen. Completed most of my academic education in Aruba, I migrated to England and completed nursing and post-graduate midwifery in four years. Met and married George in England, we migrated to America with our two daughters in 1964. In 1972, my abusive marriage ended in divorce. Given custody of our four daughters, I dare not take them, for their father chose to indulge in heavy witchcraft, and threatened to end their lives if I were to take them.

To maintain my sanity, I attended the City University of New York and continued after the divorce. Also, I started missionary work and kept busy on the mission field for many years while I continued to focus on the promises of God and what He says in His Word. The Scripture reads, "For I know the thoughts that I think toward you, says the LORD, thoughts of peace, and not of evil, to give you an expected end" (Jeremiah 29: 11). In other words, God's plan for you is to prosper you and not to harm you, to give you hope and a future. I think of this hope as I experienced constant harassment for many years following the divorce, even today. I want to encourage the readers of this book that regardless of what is happening in your life, God is your deliverer. I can attest to the fact that even though the Lord was not high on my list of priorities, there was always a sense of knowing that Jesus was more than just going to church on Sunday mornings for one hour. There was a sense of knowing, a sense of longing for more than a Sunday session. I could not talk about it but there was this tugging in my spirit, a sense of knowing there was something missing. I felt a deep sense of emptiness in my heart. As I matured in the Lord, it became obvious that all I needed was to get a hold of the Word of God, read it, study it, meditate on it, and make it my daily meal. So, when all hell breaks loose and life throws a dangerous cloud all around you, don't let that discourage you from moving towards the destination God has for you. It is an education in itself and a challenge of a lifetime. In fact, life is a challenge and it is worth holding on tightly by looking at the positive side, reading the Word of God. In doing so, you give the enemy a black eye. I have decided that I will not throw in the towel. Instead, I plan to use every ounce of energy so that God's plan for me will materialize. You might be in an abusive situation and feel God can no longer use you. That is not so.

Even after I have escaped the horror of being in bed with the abuser, he refuses to give up. But God has instilled in my heart a great moment of triumph, and I am holding on to that. The Scripture says, "Trust in the Lord with all your heart and lean not unto your own understanding: In all your ways acknowledge him, and he shall direct your paths" (Proverbs 3:5, 6). This means, regardless of what the enemy throws in your path, stay focus on God's promises. He is a miracle worker and a deliverer. God cannot lie. He is known as Jehovah Elohim, the Creator. One who takes nothing and makes something. We are all pregnant with possibilities. So if He gives you a promise or a dream, know that He will fulfill it. Go after your dream. Your willingness to push when your labor pains are strong enough will place God in a position to move with you and for you. In my case, dreams came easily and regularly. I did not understand every dream, but I made a note of them in a book. This note book is filled with Scriptures and songs from the Lord. Entering an abusive relationship, even though I knew and experienced that kind of treatment before marriage just did not make sense. However, in my mind there was always the possibility that marriage would change things for the better. Sometimes one is of the opinion that marrying such a man would fix everything, even though all evidence points to the contrary. I can assure you it was a terrible mistake. My spouse was always sorry for his behavior, and I was always ready to forgive. But there comes a time when it can be overbearing.

When God is orchestrating your life, nothing should hinder the outcome of your dream. Mind you, the enemy will try vigorously to stop the flow of your progress, but the victory is in your perseverance. I refuse to give up. I will not give in! With God at my side I will hold on and let Him fight my battle. Whatever it takes hold on to the Word of God, and apply every promise to your life. The Scripture is a powerful weapon. It says, "It is good for me that I have been afflicted that I might learn your precepts" (Psalm 119:71). That is not unreasonable; it is the Word of God. You can meditate on it and be prepared to apply it to your life at the appropriate time.

God sees and knows what is happening to you on a daily basis. He will accomplish what He sets out to do in your life if you let Him. He looks for those who will take seriously the dreams and visions He has placed in our hearts. All we have to do is put our faith and trust in Him. Faith according to the Scripture is "The substance of things hoped for and the evidence of things not seen" (Hebrews 11:1). This means, believing God with all your heart despite your circumstances. The important thing is to stay close to the Lord so that He can empower you to carry out your dream. Now, I no longer have to sort out my dreams because the Lord makes them clear. It is up to me to follow through with His promises. One dream was very clear. The Lord asked me to write and get back to the music. Doing both was a heavy task for me.

I get on the piano, not as much as I should. I do so when I am tired after a hectic day. This certainly is unacceptable to God, but I am trying to do better by practicing more frequently.

Sometimes the storms of life try to afflict you, but be encouraged. God will not leave you comfortless. Stay in His presence and feed on His Word. You will experience His love. King David understood this well when he said, "My heart is fixed, O God, my heart is fixed: I will sing and give praise" (Psalm 57:7). Therefore, as the fiery darts come, we can take refuge in God. Sing praises and worship Him on a daily basis, and before your daily chores. Make sure He is first on your daily agenda.

According to the Scripture, God created marriage for keeps. Jesus teaches that divorce should not be an alternative simply because you can't get along. And so one person puts it this way, since the Bible says it is not good for one to be alone, there are a number of miserable people on the earth who are not single, because the law says stick with it!

Also, the Bible teaches, "For this cause shall a man leave his father and mother and cleave to his wife. And they two shall be one flesh. What therefore God has joined together let no man put asunder" (Mark 10:7-9). And if a women shall put away her husband and be married to another she commits adultery" (Mark 10:10-11). This was God's intention from the beginning.

However, the devil stepped in and caused havoc in the homes, especially in the marriage. For this reason, I share some thoughts on abusive marriage and how this abuse can persist even after the divorce, through witchcraft. Nonetheless, you can escape great danger when you invite Jesus into your life. Praise God.

CHAPTER 1

A Childhood view

Born in the Island of Grenada, first of seven children, my life was an interesting one. My parents' dwelling place was with Grandma. Grandma's house was active, two-story building. Six children grew up in that home while our parents were traveling back and forth to Trinidad and Aruba to ensure a better life for the family. From that traveling my last brother, the seventh child, was born in Trinidad.

A small Island in the Caribbean, Grenada is known as the Land of Spice, a very productive place with fertile soil. Growing up on the Island, I was not aware of the nutritional benefits and the impact it had on my life and the lives of my family. The idea that those plants and soils were valuable for one's health was unimaginable. The minerals in the soil were so rich, even today. Fruits and vegetables, green and ripe bananas, star-apples, avocadoes, citrus, ginger, saffron, cocoa, spices such as cinnamon, cloves and various other herbal plants, to name a few, are the products of the Islands. Those in the Caribbean Islands are blessed with these elements, but as a child I didn't realize the value of these foods. My concern was mainly on having note books, pen and pencil, and all the other necessities for school, as opposed to eating well.

Even as a child, I knew exactly what I wanted to eat. That did not include foods with proper nutritional value. My parents migrated to Trinidad and very often sent flour, rice and the finer things that dressed the pantry. As a result, I objected to eating the foods with the natural mineral contents, such as the leafy vegetables and those that we dig up from the earth. Where food is concerned I was very selective and demanded rice and dumpling. Although my grandmother did not adhere to my requests, that did not deter me from being persistent. Even though the whip or belt was always within reach for a good flogging, I did not have the sense to know that regardless of my complaints, Grandma would ignore my plea for different choice of foods. My parents sent foods in abundance from Trinidad, why should I eat plantain, green banana, potato and yam, when I can have a plate of rice and peas? Of course, I would have to wait until Sunday for that was especially planned for Sunday's dinner. Today, I realize the importance of the foods to which I once objected, and look desperately in the grocery stores for green bananas and other plant foods.

My parents migrated to Aruba from Trinidad, and continued to send foods and other personal items for the household. Today, in some of the affluent countries, there is so much concern about health issues as multitudes cannot afford health insurance. Despite the nutritional education here in America, obesity seems to be prevalent for good nutrition does not take priority in the dietary department at home. Recently, however, individuals are becoming more aware of the need for proper nutrition. This is a good thing.

An encounter with the unexpected

As children growing up in that home, we must travel a short distance to get water. The Pipe stand was about one mile from the house. Today, it is a pleasure to have water coming directly into the house. We did not have roads from the house, just a narrow path which led to a passage in the midst of a cocoa plantation. It was dark and deserted but did not pose a problem. Daily we were assigned to fetch water from the pipe. Using a container with a handle, we carried it on our heads or held it in our hands. It was sometimes easier to carry it on our heads. That was usually the task of the older children.

We loved traveling to the pipe stand where we could meet some of the neighborhood children. Our house seemed secluded from everything and everybody. It was on a hill where we could see some of the activities, but that was not enough. We wanted to meet the other children.

At ten years old, it was my assignment and it has never been a difficult task, partly because we were able to meet and talk to the children in the neighborhood. Our house was away from the hustle and bustle, so it was a welcome treat to take a trip to the pipe stand on a regular basis. Crime was not part of the territory. In fact, crime was unheard of in the Island. However, this morning was a set up by the atmospheric presence of the unknown.

A teenager, son of the neighborhood baker, about sixteen years old, was in the vicinity and demanded that I lay down. Gasped for a breath, fear gripped me to my bones as he took my hand, laid me down on a smooth path then proceeded to remove his pants. Realizing what he was about to do, I yelled at the top of my voice. He took off instantly and ran away.

Full speed, I hurried home to report the incident to Mother. She accompanied me to the young man's mother, a hard working baker in the community. In the midst of putting bread in the oven, she stopped and listened to my mother's complaint. In the presence of my mother and me, she gave her son a severe flogging while he humbly accepted his punishment. That was an isolated incident and my assignment to fetch water from the pipe continued. It was the first and last time something like this occurred on the Island as far as I know.

Punishing Rod

Liberated with the belt and whip, my parents made full use of that when condition arose. Even though they meant well, the punishments were at times too severe. Daddy's anger during the deliverance of a flogging at times contributed to some physical damage. We did not complain, and there was no one to whom we could report. In fact, we knew that would only escalate the punishment. They admitted those punishments were for our good. To be honest, when we looked at the situation of our schoolmates many years later, after returning from Aruba, we realized the floggings kept us in good moral standing in the community, if only they were a little less severe. Of course, we always did something to warrant a spanking. On that side of the world, growing up with strict parents who had full control of the belt and whip, it was imperative to stand and take the punishment that was rightfully yours. Nonetheless, anytime such an occasion arose, the thought of a flogging was so frightening I would freeze.

One morning Mother was about to chastise me, but I played hide and seek all day. I was terribly afraid of the whip. Even though I cannot remember what my offense was, I have a vivid memory of the beating. I call it a beating. Flogging is too mild a word for this kind of punishment. I lingered outside of the house and would not go inside. Deep down in my soul I knew Mother would not give up on me. The longer I dodged the worse it was going to be. However, in my mind I said, "This body cannot take this kind of punishment today."

The river was about one mile from the house. At a young age of ten years old, my assignment was before me. As a result, I took a trip to the river to do some washing. (Normally we washed on a large stone in the river, as this was the place where we did most of the washings. Taking pleasure in washing, rubbing the clothes on the stone, making sure they were clean was a fun thing).

Suddenly, a hand grabbed my arm. I shuddered! It was Mother. She held on to me, led me along the path on the way home without saying a word. Trembling, fear gripped me to my bones. At this point she was angry, as you could imagine. I was thinking of the worse, justifiably so. You think there was no need for me to fear? Hold on to your seats. We are home. Mother tied my hands behind my back, put a rope around my waist, and with my hands secured with the rope, she tied me to a large pole outside of the house. She gave me a beating to remember all of my life. Now do you get the picture?

Playing hide and seek was the worst thing a child should attempt in my parents' home when punishment was imminent. I know that now. Let me tell you something. I never again dare to attempt running or hiding for the rest of my life. Grandma was usually around to plead our case.

She could not do anything about this—not this time. Complaining about this type of punishment was out of the question. Today, especially in America, this is physical abuse which must be reported to the authorities. For example, you cannot prevent the child from reporting the incident. If the child does not complain, the teacher has a responsibility to observe and notify the appropriate authority. Mind you, did our parents love us? Absolutely! They wanted the best for us. Consequently, in their eyes they were doing what was right in order to keep us on the right path. They were training us to have good character. What a depiction of love! This was before my parents began to travel abroad, first to Trinidad, then to Aruba.

In thinking back on this particular punishment, I try to recall what I had done at the time. Would you believe I simply cannot recall the reason for the punishment? I know it was something simple, requiring a scolding or counseling. Scolding or counseling was not in my parents' mode of thinking. Even though this would suffice most of the time, there was no reasoning such as discussing the issue. The belt or whip would do the speaking. That was the only solution as far as they were concerned.

In addition, whenever punishment was imminent, especially by Daddy, everybody ought to get out of the way, because the belt was no respect of person. Everyone who was in the way during the flogging of another would also get a taste of the pie. There was neither mercy nor compromise. At the age of ten, remembering this so vividly, I would assume it would have some effect on me mentally, but I don't think that was so because I was able to study with no problems at school or in graduate programs. My siblings and I were subject to our parents' demands without being disrespectful. We dare not complain or give vent to our feelings.

Despite the severity of the punishment, our parents did not consider that excessive or unusual disciplinary action. As far as they were concerned it was the most constructive means of correction, or the most honorable thing to do. To reiterate, they meant well and wanted the best for us. They demanded respect, and we honored them despite the severity of the punishments.

Traveling lends mercy

There was a new sense of hope, a sense of belonging to a new era, as my parents began to travel extensively. The change was evident as they traveled to and from Trinidad, each time bringing fine foods and gifts. We looked forward to Mother's returning with gifts and things that we loved. My uncle resided in Trinidad, so my parents were no stranger to the Island. Blessed with a job, Daddy worked with the Oil Company and Mother joined him there. She left us with Grandmother.

To reiterate, the great thing about the soil in the Caribbean is that it is laden with minerals. The foods we grow, though high in carbohydrates are free of chemicals. Green banana is complex carbohydrate. This means it is low calorie, high in potassium, natural sugars, vitamin A, B, iron and phosphorus. The glycemic index of bananas varies depending on how ripe they are. As a result, green bananas are good for diabetics. Nonetheless, portions are important. It is a good source of fiber, and because of the abundance of vitamins and minerals, bananas are a great source of natural energy. The potassium content in bananas helps the body's circulatory system and delivers oxygen to the brain. The leafy vegetables such as dasheen bush, lettuce and so on are healthy foods without chemicals or pesticides. Rice, flour and the other bagged foods were part of the diet used mostly on a Sunday, a day for special banquet.

My parents continued to send much of the bagged foods from Trinidad, such as rice and flour. My siblings and I were elated and wished we could eat rice and dumpling more often. However, they were more tolerable than I. In fact, I objected to the vegetables and foods that were high in minerals. If there was nothing else in the house the choice was limited to the natural plantation foods. I wanted to eat much more of the processed foods that my parents sent from Trinidad. Rice and flour were special to me. I rebelled and cried at meal times. It was not fair to feed me with those vegetation foods when my parents were sending other foods from Trinidad. I had no idea those home-grown foods were good nourishment for the body, free of pesticides and other harmful contaminants. I now realize those foods were what kept my brain functioning well, even today. Mother came home from Trinidad often and looked beautiful. I can remember admiring my mother each time she came home. She was tall, well-built, beautiful woman, whose dress code was outstanding. Mother became a dress designer and designed our clothes. My siblings and I were dressed alike going to church services, and were commended by the people whenever we were together. Before Mother began to travel, she clothed us in flour-bag dresses. My youngest sisters had no experience with flour-bag dresses. For those who are not familiar with flour bags, let me explain. In grocery shopping, my parents bought large bags of flour, then washed and bleached the bags and used them to design dresses for my siblings and me. They were not well fitting as far as I could remember, and I believed every-body knew they were made from flour bags. That lasted until Mother became a professional dress designer.

The grass is never greener on the other side

At about eleven years old, now living with Daddy's parents, life was somewhat different and the home was not conducive to healthy living, spiritually. Grandmother had three daughters at home and the youngest one was a lesbian. How did I know this? She approached me. Even though I was the tender age of 11, I realized what she was trying to do was not right . . . She was an adult, probably in her twenties, overly friendly and kind to me. Nonetheless, I did not like the food and demonstrated this in my attitude at meal times. I was able to get out of that atmosphere quickly. Mother came home from Trinidad and moved me to another parish, the parish of St. David, to live with my aunt and her family.

CHAPTER 2

Another get-away

Here at St. David's parish, a new environment and new school setting with my aunt, her husband and 3 children. I was a long way from my siblings, but was intrigued to have my ninety-four year-old great grandmother near to me. She was about one minute from my aunt. I experienced no drama in the dietary department. Everything seemed to be working well. What made the difference? Although rice and flour were not part of the food preparation, the variety was good. This included pea soup with vegetables such as breadfruit, dumpling, green bananas and so on. The difference was in the variety of foods.

More importantly, it was probably God's plan that I got away from that last environment. My great grandmother was within easy access. She spoke broken French and I loved her. Trying to understand the language was fun. My aunt's daughter spoke the language fluently because she was born in that environment. One important factor in grasping another language is to live in the area. In parts of the Caribbean Island, some of the older people spoke broken French, especially when they didn't want you to understand what they were saying. Here I had the opportunity to grasp another dialogue, even though it's broken French.

With my parents traveling, we always seemed to be moving to different schools, causing us to fall behind in our class work. Nonetheless, I loved St. David's parish. Mother arranged for private, after-school lessons for me. The teacher was very patient, and taught in the elementary school where I attended regularly. I did an after-school session with him once a week, doing mathematics and English Grammar. He was a tremendous help to me.

Another move to try my integrity

One afternoon after school, I was alone in the house. My aunt's husband pulled me into the bedroom. At the age of 12, I fought him with every ounce of strength God gave me. He left me alone, unhurt. Later, when I recalled that encounter I considered myself strong in the Lord. Of course, this was what good nutrition did for us. It was not obvious until later on in life, that a good diet was essential for children. This includes nutritionally sound doctrine. The Scripture says, "Train up a child in the way he should go: and when he is old, he will not depart from it" (Proverbs 22:6). My aunt's daughter came in and I related the whole scenario to her, who in turn, related it to Great Grandmother.

My Aunt came home from the field and both her daughter and Great Grandmother related the incident to her. I, personally, did not have to do much talking. My aunt was a fireball. She made no joke. She took the situation in hand, got hold of her husband and the rest was history. I continued to live in peace right there in that home. My uncle made no further attempt to touch me. He respected me from here on and things continued normally. With the strong warning and threat by his wife, he had to pull his socks up. My aunt demonstrated her love for me over her own daughter because I was a very obedient child. Whatever she required of me, I humbly surrendered without murmuring or complaining. Nothing was too difficult for me to do. She spent much time in the field while I often found myself alone in the house after school.

Alone in the house another time and hungry, I looked around the kitchen for something to eat. The only thing available to me was some raw meat. The family had killed a pig, and the meat was fresh and looked healthy. Although it would take a long time to cook, I cut a piece of the pork and placed it in a pan on the stove. It was one of those outside stove requiring wood to keep it functioning. That was already in place. It was easy to just slip a piece of raw meat in a container and cook it on the burner. Of course pork would not cook in a hurry but I was hopeful. With a little luck it would be ready before my aunt got home.

Oops! My aunt is home. The cooking is not complete.

"Who put this meat on the stove?" She inquired.

Nobody knew. I kept silent. My aunt had a mysterious way of finding out the culprit. She proceeded to the test. Confident that I was innocent, she questioned her three children and the report came back negative. She continued with the test and found out I was the guilty one. That was the first time I experienced a much deserved spanking from my loving aunt.

It would have been easy to say, "Yes Aunty, I was hungry." I believed if I had confessed she would not be angry, because she appreciated me, as a willing and obedient child. I was ashamed to have her come from gardening to find the uncooked meat on the stove. As the guilty person, I received the just punishment.

Parents on the move again

My parents completed their assignments in Trinidad and ready to migrate to Aruba, Netherlands Antilles. They came home from Trinidad and prepared to travel again. They left for Aruba and continued to send food and other gifts for the whole family, including my cousins, my aunt's children. I was separated from my siblings temporarily.

After two years at St. David, I was ready to travel with my siblings. Our parents arranged to have us join them in Aruba. We were elated with the idea. Even though this was going to be another school setting with a different culture and language, we looked forward to the move. Despite the harsh punishments we received at their hands, we were simply overwhelmed with joy to join them. We didn't hold a grudge against them for the floggings we received, because we learned much as a result. They really felt that they were justified, and the punishments were to show that they wanted the best for us. We accepted their reasoning with humility.

It was 1947, bells rang throughout the Island. "War is over, war is over!" That was the alarm. I did not understand what was going on, but whatever it was there was some excitement in the air. World War II was over and my siblings and I were getting ready to travel for the first time. It was an historical landmark I will never forget.

We left Grenada for Aruba at the end of World War II, and must first make a stop in transit. Very excited, we left Grenada by boat to Trinidad where we spent a few days with family. Before boarding the plane for Aruba my aunt introduced us to Trinidad. We loved the Island and were scheduled to leave on Carnival Monday morning. Carnival is a very special celebration in Trinidad even today. People travel from all over the world to attend this festival. Nonetheless, we were scheduled to leave Trinidad on that special day. The day before we were to leave there was a knock on the door. KLM flight personnel came with a question.

"You are scheduled to leave for Aruba in the morning, but if you want to stay for carnival we will gladly change the flight. Would you like to experience carnival tomorrow?" They inquired.

"No, we want to leave tomorrow." All agreed.

"Are you sure? Carnival is beautiful." They insisted.

We believed seeing our parents took priority over carnival. In fact, we were young and had no idea what carnival really meant. Nothing was more important than joining our parents. Not realizing the real significance of that festival, we declined to stay.

It's Monday morning and we are off to the airport to begin our flight to Aruba. Our parents were waiting for us. We were excited and couldn't wait to get there. The flight took off, our first experience on a plane. What an excitement. My siblings and I were of one mind in the decision to leave on Carnival Monday. The flight took off beautifully. We looked out of the plane, the sky was blue, clear, and clouds were minimal. The ride was smooth with no bumps in the air. We arrived safely in Aruba. Thank God.

Would you believe this? Friends and neighbors could not believe we were in Aruba on Carnival Monday.

"Why didn't you stay for carnival?" One of the neighbors asked.

We were just finding out how we missed something special. What's more, our parents would have had no problem with our staying for carnival. Even though KLM personnel tried to convince us, we had no idea how important that was. Our young minds directed us to meet our parents as priority. I cannot remember my parents ever commenting on carnival. Nonetheless, as we matured, we hear so much about carnival in Trinidad, and people would come from all over the globe to experience the carnival celebration.

Settling down and getting acquainted with the new school I saw new challenges in a strange environment. St. Theresa's Roman Catholic School with a friendly atmosphere, Dutch was going to be the new language. We found out that it was mandatory to speak Dutch in the classrooms and on the school premises. Intuitively, English was extremely important to me. As I looked on those days, I believed even then God had a plan for me. A good grip on the English language was part of that plan. I can assure you, whatever your plans are, English language is an asset. You must believe that, or you would soon wish you had placed much emphasis on the English language during your school years.

Today, children will find it invaluable as a required subject. Take my word for it. Even though learning a new language was important, I realized that in the end a good English background would pay off later in life. I took care of that by enrolling in an English course from England while I was in Aruba. I thank God for giving me that inspiration as a teenager and with the help of my mother, who obviously envisioned where the Lord was taking me, prompted me to go on by adding after-school sessions to my curriculum which included Typing and Shorthand.

Music Industry

Here in Aruba, Mother enrolled me in piano lessons with a private teacher. The preference was classical music. To the teacher, good fingering was an asset, and I had problem with that. I simply could not get the fingering right. Bad fingering was unacceptable. Consequently, she often used a ruler or a stick on my fingers whenever I failed to keep them in an upright position. That was a terrible experience. She indicated that I would not succeed in music unless my fingering was perfect. After about two years, my mother assigned me to another teacher. She was a young woman my age group whose method of teaching was slightly different, and she was more lenient in terms of fingering. She made teaching enjoyable.

After school program

To reiterate, Mother enrolled me in Stenography school—Shorthand and Typing. I graduated with 55 words per minute in shorthand, and 80 words in typing. Today, with the extensive writing I have been doing, the typing lesson was an asset. My parents bought me a typewriter and I loved the sound of it. Many years later, I bought an electric typewriter which served me well during my adult years, for college and post-graduate assignments.

In Aruba we were all responsible for completing home assignments. Laundry—washing, ironing, cleaning, and even school work. The girls must be able to iron Daddy's shirts perfectly, with no creases, starting with the yoke. We sprinkled the shirt with water before ironing, to make sure the well-starched shirt was done thoroughly. So, my second sister and I were competent at ironing a cotton shirt. There were no creases in the shirt at the completion of the ironing. I loved ironing. That was part of our daily chores.

We were in Aruba when the news came that Great Grandmother died suddenly. Ninety-five years old Grandmother was always busy working in the garden. One morning while she was on her regular duty, someone accidentally hit her with a stone. She became disabled, and died. That news came as a surprise because she seemed so strong and didn't need assistance to walk or move around. She neither suffered with arthritis nor any other diseases. When I left Grenada she was in perfect health. Obviously, her time had come to go home to be with the Lord.

CHAPTER 3

Time for change

Having completed some of my academic education, I secured a job at a hardware store employed as a cashier and sales person. Daddy worked with an Oil and Transport Company in Aruba, an American firm. After many years of service he was laid off and returned to Grenada, having bought an estate from a previous owner. So, the family went home with the plan to travel again without Daddy. His desire was to settle, take care of the estate, with hired workers to assist in the house and in the field. Mother's desire was to accompany us to England.

Consequently, after seven years in Aruba, I was back in Grenada for a short stay before travelling to England. Mother kept a prayer of thanksgiving and invited the community to participate in the service. There was much prayer and food and it was a joyous occasion before leaving Grenada for the second time.

After two months in Grenada, we were ready to travel again. My siblings and I made new friends but soon had to say goodbye. We prepared to leave with Mother who was not willing to settle in Grenada at that time. Daddy had no intention of traveling again. My two sisters and I would begin our nursing education in England. One of my brothers joined us on the journey. After saying goodbye to friends, Daddy and the rest of the family, we got ourselves ready to move again.

Long journey at sea

July 1954 we left Grenada via Trinidad for England. Our second visit to Trinidad, as matured individuals we had a better understanding of the Island. After spending three months with Mother's family and learned much about the Island, we were on our way to the United Kingdom.

September 1954, we left Trinidad by the ship, "S.S. Hildebrand," for England. We boarded the ship with other young ladies traveling to England. Three young ladies boarded the ship from Saint Vincent, and one from Trinidad, to begin nursing education as well. Such a long trip by sea, the experience was enjoyable and worth every moment of it. In addition to singing various songs, the young lady from Trinidad was a great story teller. Very creative, she was fun to be with. We enjoyed her stories. The ship's cook was friendly, the food tasty, and everyone enjoyed it. I did not experience sea sickness, and that added to the pleasurable mood on board.

After 21 days at sea, we arrived at Liverpool, England. The weather was terribly cold, foggy and damp. For the first time we were about to experience some bitter cold weather. However, my mother's presence made a huge difference after we arrived in such weather condition. Mother's uncle met us at the Pierre and we spent some time with him until we secured our own place. Years later, Uncle died of Tetanus. He had a chicken farm and his finger became infected, but sought medical advice too late.

First winter experience, London was an interesting place. The subway, the historical buildings, including Buckingham Palace, all seemed so interesting. Even though there was no central heating at our place at the time, the living condition was tolerable. Today, it is a completely different environment.

My siblings and I secured a job at a toy factory for three months before we began our nursing education. The job entailed sitting down at a table and painting metal toys. Actually, they were figurines. We sat together at the same table and sang all the way to the closing of the session. We simply enjoyed what we were doing, from September to December. The employers appreciated us. We wanted to acquaint ourselves with the job industry, and that was a good setting while we did our entrance examination for the nursing profession.

January 1955 I began my nursing education. My younger sibling was too young to begin general nursing. (You must be 18 years old). However, she was accepted at an Eye Institution. After two years she graduated with a Diploma in Ophthalmic nursing, and proceeded to general nursing for another two years. This was an asset for her to be able to fulfill those two aspects of nursing in four years. After 2 years, she graduated a Registered Professional Nurse.

My other sibling chose to study outside of London, a beautiful, quiet area of England. I chose to stay in London and began my training at Whittington Hospital, North of London. Anatomy and physiology were the most challenging in the nursing profession.

However, I met other students from Jamaica with whom I was able to study. Becoming acquainted with them was an asset. Studying became less stressful. We met every day after school to study. One day we tackled anatomy and physiology, another time we attempted specific sections of the body such as the heart, and its' location, and every other organ in the body; then the bones and their function, and so on.

Group study lessens the tension and makes it easier to sit at an exam. My choice of study was originally music but my mother made the decision for me. As a student of music, I had indicated to her that I would like to study music in England. Her reply to me was, "Not a bit of it, you will study nursing!" I have not regretted it, though. I was able to work on some of my music, even though anatomy and physiology were quite challenging. I had no regret residing at the nursing hostel because I had full access to the piano. Also, all those fellow students resided there as well.

During the interview, the matron gave me a choice to live in the nurses' residence or live outside of the hospital premises. I consented to live at the residence, away from home and the rest of the family, so that I was able to concentrate on my studies. More encouraging, the matron in charge of the hostel loved to hear me play. She challenged me to go on and made frequent mention of her love for my musical skill.

Extracurricular activities

A short train ride took me to Earl's Court in London. The place is called The Students' Center of Earl's Court. Students of various learning gathered there for entertainment and fellowship. One evening I accepted an invitation to visit the Center. Accompanied by a friend I visited the center, about 15 minutes ride on the subway. It was imperative that I return to the hostel at or before 11 PM, sign the register and head to my room. With that in mind, I made sure the entertainment didn't take all my attention. I enjoyed my first visit at the center.

The season's festival began and I was invited to a Christmas party at the Center. I met George from Grenada who lived in Earl's Court. He was pleasant, handsome and talkative. After a few months he proposed and I accepted his proposal. Later he demonstrated an attitude of extreme jealousy with a vile tempter for no obvious reason. Nonetheless, I was blinded by his outward demeanor and continued the relationship, hoping he would change that insanely jealous attitude. At the time I found out he was seeing another young lady. However, he indicated to me that was not a viable relationship. That certainly was a warning sign. I soon became trapped with the sweet talk. As a gullible young lady, I was ready to soak up whatever he placed in front of me without question.

As the relationship grew, what I noticed in his jealous character was an abusive person, both verbally and physically. Yet he was always apologizing for his atrocious behavior. As a forgiving person, I was always ready to accept his plea for mercy. That, again, should have indicated to me that something was terribly wrong mentally. Incapable of detecting an inherent abusive nature in an individual, I continued the relationship with him. In the midst of his charm there was an ongoing jealousy and verbal abuse for no apparent reason. In public he was the most charming individual. No one would believe the real character behind that charm.

Nursing education a priority

My nursing education was a priority as every other activity became secondary. After three months of preliminary training, the students were placed on the units to care for live patients. The teachers assigned two students to each unit. My first unit was a male medical unit with 30 patients. Entering the unit, an Irish nurse and I were two newcomers from preliminary training school, (PTS) to start our first encounter with live patients, as opposed to working with mannequins. Trying to put on a face of confidence, we strolled along the unit. The patients were inquisitive, looking directly at us as the ward sister introduced and gave us the report of each patient.

My first challenge on the unit came when the ward sister handed me a syringe in a kidney dish. "Nurse, give this injection to Mr. John Doe." (Not his real name). She said with confidence. Looking at her with amazement, my eyes must have indicated that I was not ready for that kind of assignment. "Just pinch the arm and inject him under the skin." She said. "Go on you can do it." She insisted. I had much practice in the classrooms using a mannequin. Now I face the real challenge, live encounter with patients. Headed for the patient's bed, I tried not to show any sign of anxiety. After checking the patient's name I administered the injection hypodermically—under the skin. Well done.

Classroom instructions continued on a regular basis on assigned days, so that the ward sister knew when to expect us on the unit. Training, both in classrooms and personal encounter with the patients, was amazing. It was an experience to know that you are in a position to work with sick people. More so, to watch them recover and go home was a rewarding experience. The nurse's function was to be able to detect objectively and subjectively what was going on with a patient. Objective observation is what you, the nurse, observe. Subjective is what the patient or client describes to you. For example, what he is experiencing personally. Objective and subjective symptoms are important requirements in concluding a diagnosis.

Preparing for the first big examination

Preliminary examination after the first year gave the students an idea how the final exam was going to affect us. We worked hard and studied rigorously every evening as a group. After the second year things got a little better as we prepared for the final examination. Anatomy and physiology continued to be a challenge. We often had mini examination in the classrooms on a weekly basis. That was extremely helpful, for it calmed my nerves for the big ones. Although examinations were never a joy to me, each time I sat at an examination table at the institution, it released some of the built-up tension before the State examination. After three years of practical training, the nursing examination took place in two parts. Written examination came first, then the practical examination on the hospital premises.

In England, the nurses were responsible for doing most of the laboratory tests on urine. For example, urinalysis consists of testing for protein—albumen, sugar, acetone and blood in the urine. Those were routine tests that the nurses handled on the units daily. As the nurses' responsibility, we had to demonstrate that during the practical examination while the examiner stood and evaluated us on the spot.

In addition, the final examination included general hygiene, hand-washing technique, preparing to bathe a patient in bed and much more. Those were parts of the practical examination. Three years of hard work consisted of working on various units. As students, we moved from medical to surgical units, pediatric units, orthopedic units, to gynecological units. Maternity and premature nursery, were specialty areas. My heart was leading me to those specialty areas as a permanent home after graduation. I loved the maternity department.

We moved from white uniform to green stripe with an apron. The third year, we were dressed in navy blue. Finally, after much training theory and practical experience under supervision, we were ready for the final exam. That included two parts, practical and theoretical, for the hospital. The state examination followed on another date. We made it. What a relief! Promoted to navy blue uniforms, black belt with silver buckle, we demonstrated that the hard work paid off. Thank God. I made many friends, coming to the U.K. on the boat, and during my nurse training at the hospital, with whom I was able to study. Generally, studying together is rewarding. It pays off tremendously. In my experience as a nurse trainee, I couldn't do it without the group's help. Things I didn't understand in the classrooms, group study helped to clarify them accurately. After three years of much work and study, we graduated as State Registered Nurse (SRN).

CHAPTER 4

Yearly evaluation

To reiterate, during my midwifery training, I worked on every unit. My favorite department was the premature nursery. What intrigued me was the adequacy in administering oxygen to the tiny infants, in an attempt to save their lives and avoid damage to the retina of the eye; a condition that happened occasionally due to excessive oxygen supply to the infants while they are in the incubator. I loved this aspect of nursing, and the time for my annual evaluation is to be revealed.

The unit Sister does an evaluation and sends to Matron's office. Every year Matron calls the student nurses to her office to discuss their evaluation. You never know what kind of evaluation you receive until you are called to the office. However, because I was a hard, efficient worker, I always felt confident that my evaluation would speak for me in that capacity. The time came for my evaluation report after working on various units. The Matron called me to the office.

I sat in Matron's office while she read each report from various units. One evaluation was really out-standing. Matron's remark was, "This is the kind of evaluation to have, nurse." That was a great encouragement for me to know that the head of those departments recognized my daily performances. It pays to work well in whatever you do.

A large request of me

Sister on one of the surgical units came from Guy's hospital in London. Those from Guy's are known as the prejudice folks. However, Sister requested that I work as her assistant after graduation. She was not a favorite, but I found no fault with her. We worked well together. In fact, I was able to work well with everybody. As a student nurse, that unit was one of my assigned areas. Some of my fellow workers asked me not to accept the position.

However, the request was in Matron's office and I had no intention of refusing the position. Mind you, it was as a result of my working with her as a student she was able to make that determination. I was happy to accept the appointment because we got along well together. She did not tolerate laziness and I could relate to that. Her attitude was not appealing to many of the staff members because she was very strict and did not tolerate nonsense.

Sister turned out to be a great person to work with. Although people appreciated me for my hard work, it was such a joy being able to function with integrity and good character without looking at the clock. I was a perfectionist. Everything must be in order before signing off duty. I enjoyed the position thoroughly. On her off day, I was in charge of the unit of 30 plus patients. It was a well deserved experience before embarking on my midwifery training.

After one year in that capacity, it was time to move on to another realm. In the same hospital, I applied for midwifery training. Whittington Hospital has a part I midwifery department. To practice as a midwife one had to go to a hospital that provided part II as well. Therefore, my plan to practice at my home school necessitated moving to another area in London for the second part midwifery.

Midwifery training begins

After one year of working as a staff (charge) nurse with Sister, I began part I midwifery at my home school, Whittington Hospital, midwifery department. After witnessing ten deliveries and delivering ten babies under supervision, I was assigned to work on all the other maternity units as part of my training. It was rewarding to watch those two-pound babies leave for home at five pounds, in good condition.

Completed part I midwifery training at home school, the criteria required every midwifery student witness 10 deliveries, and deliver 10 babies under supervision. I loved every moment of it, and planned to make it my specialty. This was a teaching hospital. The midwife was responsible to supervise nurses and medical students who were interested in midwifery. A great responsibility and I headed in that direction to specialize in that field. That required a complete post graduate course of one year.

Part I required six months training. Part II required six months also. I applied for Part II midwifery which included three months at the hospital at Lewisham General Hospital, and three months on the district—Queen's District Nursing Association in Woolwich, S. E. London.

Wedding Plans in the Making

George suggested we get married before beginning Part II midwifery. To reiterate, George and I met at Earl's Court Christmas party at the students' center in London. Extremely jealous with a horrible temper, a very abusive character was part of his makeup. That should wear off, I thought. The wedding date was set for August. Despite his abusive character, I took the chance and committed to the marriage vow with my eyes widely opened. Love is blind and foolish, and young women turn their eyes from the seemingly dangerous outlook because of physical attraction. I accepted the marriage proposal hoping that it was going to work well for us.

August 15, 1959, my wedding day. My mother designed the dress and my sister-in-law decorated it with beads and sequins. They did a fantastic job. My girlfriend, Gloria, sent me a beautiful tiara from New York. We met and shared an apartment in London after I moved from the hostel, then she migrated to America. The wedding happened at the Roman Catholic Church. I was a Roman Catholic, my spouse an Anglican who did not attend church but went with me after we met. The day went well with a great number of guests, including many of my co-workers. It was a beautiful occasion and a beautiful wedding. The guests had a great time at the reception.

George rented a room from one of his friends until we were able to buy our own home. We moved into that home after the wedding reception and hoped this was going to be a temporary arrangement as we shopped for our home. It was not long before he manifested his ugly side.

One evening we were having a conversation with his friend in the kitchen. Then we left to settle for the night leaving his friend in the kitchen which was close to our room. Suddenly George became violent for no reason whatever. I had no idea what transpired in the kitchen that caused him to flare up like that. I must have said something that didn't meet his approval while we were speaking. Later, in the bedroom, getting ready to have a good night's rest he abruptly exploded. Without any explanation he began to be verbally abusive. Then he proceeded to hit me. His friend was still in the kitchen and couldn't believe what he was hearing. This was very early in the marriage. How did I get myself into this? Nonetheless, he was always apologizing for his behavior, and I was ceaselessly ready to forgive him. As this abusive behavior continued, I concluded he was a sick person and encouraged him to seek counseling, but he refused each time saying, "We can work it out together."

Meanwhile, as we shopped for a home, the real estate agency presented us with many options from which to choose. Eventually we found a property with rentable space. We were fortunate and blessed to find favorable tenants. They lived comfortably and felt at home. One of them was an Indian woman from Guyana who taught me to make fruit cake, often called "black cake." You soaked the fruits in wine for many months before making the cake at Christmas. She was truly an expert in that capacity. Also, she taught me to do curried chicken. She was special, a great cook.

Leaving to complete midwifery part II

Midwifery part II began at Lewisham General Hospital. It involved moving away from home for six months. Three months at the hospital and three months on the district. After witnessing and completing the required number of deliveries at the hospital, I moved to Queens District Nursing Association in Woolwich to start training for home confinement. Not all mothers would qualify for home confinement (delivery). Yet there were those who insisted on delivering their babies at home, even though they were not qualified medically. Unless the condition was extremely grave, we would grant their requests. Of course it doesn't always materialize satisfactorily. I will explain later.

My first assignment on the district began with a strange experience. I was asleep at 3 a.m. when I heard a knock on my door. It was my supervisor, a quiet, elderly Irish nurse, very unassuming with slurred speech.

"Mrs. Preudhomme, we have a call, wake up."

I managed to hop out of the bed, a little groggy but made it after putting on my uniform. Heading out and up the hill, we walked to the home of this person who was ready to deliver her baby. Because I was not able to ride a bicycle, the midwife walked with me. Normally everyone on the district rides a bicycle or drives a car. I got my share of exercise from walking to and from the job. (As a young lady in Aruba, I made many attempts to ride a bicycle with no success. Each time I mounted the bicycle I fell. So I gave it up).

Grab on to your seats

I was not too excited about getting out of bed at 3 a.m. for my first assignment. However, once outside I was refreshed, just to think I was about to have my first home delivery on the district. We arrived at the home to prepare the mother for her delivery. A woman let us in and guided us to the bedroom only to find a deceased male in the bed. With a quiet, slurred voice, the midwife said, "Let's lay him out, we are here already."

During midwifery practices, the procedure was not to touch the dead while handling maternity patients. However, we were on the spot and needed to do the obvious. After straightening the body, we went back to the hostel and notified the appropriate organization on the district, so they could take care of the body. I showered and went back to bed. After a few hours I got up, refreshed myself, and headed for breakfast. The Director remarked, "I hear you had a strange experience this morning." I had no idea whether or not I should smile or laugh. I chose to remain quiet without uttering a word.

Following that experience I began my normal function, to visit all the ante partum/prenatal mothers before delivery. After doing this on a daily basis, I decided that was where I wanted to be. No one was ready for delivery, but I continued to check on the status of each mother to make sure her blood pressure was stable and normal, and that she understood the procedure for home confinement. Hoping that I would be assigned to a supervisor who would take the messages accurately in the future, I went to bed at nights and slept comfortably.

Second Call

Another supervisor was on duty when my second call came. Very alert, professional, typical British individual, I was assigned to her permanently. She drove a car. My second call came at a decent hour from a mother who was beginning to experience labor pains.

I accompanied the supervisor who checked the status of the mother. Labor was advancing rapidly and she was ready to deliver her baby. The supervisor spent some time with the patient then left me to carry on with the delivery. To reiterate, not every mother on the district would qualify for home confinement.

Even though this mother was not a good candidate for home confinement, she insisted on having her baby at home. Her hemoglobin was 7.0 mgs percent and was considered anemic. One's hemoglobin should be at least 10 mgs percent with a normal blood pressure, to be considered a good candidate for home confinement. Hemoglobin of 7.0 mgs percent was certainly un-acceptable. Her third child, delivery was likely to proceed rapidly. Despite her blood report, we hoped all would be well for mother and baby.

Everything went well and I delivered a healthy baby boy. I handed the baby to the father so he could bond with him for a few minutes before placing him in the basinet. The third stage of delivery in progress with some probable delay. The uterus was not contracting, and there was no sign of the placenta/afterbirth. I administered the required medication to help the uterus to contract. However, the uterus remained sluggish, and the patient began to bleed excessively. I gave her a dose of morphine and asked the husband to call the supervisor.

Meanwhile I prepared the mother for transfer to the hospital. The supervisor arrived, and I accompanied mother and baby to the hospital via ambulance. This was one example of taking a chance on home confinement when all evidence proved possible fatality. Despite the mother's refusal to comply at the onset, she ended up in the hospital during the third stage of the delivery. After an uneventful delivery, both mother and baby went home in good condition. The home care continued on a daily basis. My assignment was to supervise breast-feeding and general hygiene of both mother and baby. Midwifery practice continued uneventful, with no further incident. In my possession is the photograph of my first delivery on the district—1960. I cherish it.

A surprise visit

My husband visited me on the district unannounced. We were newlyweds, but I had to be away for section two of midwifery training. The Director made a statement to him.

"Your wife does not have a sense of humor." She said.

She was right because I couldn't laugh at all the jokes they made at the dining table. In fact, even as a young woman I was always serious. I simply could not laugh at everything. I assumed that was not normal or acceptable to those around me. My husband went back home to North London. Lewisham was the South East area of London, a long way from home. The rest of my journey was uneventful. It was a good experience while it lasted and I planned to use midwifery as my nursing specialty. The midwifery department included premature nursery, mother and baby care, labor and delivery department. I was happy to be back at home school, Whittington Hospital Maternity Department, to practice as a qualified midwife. That included teaching nursing students and medical students who were interested in midwifery practice.

CHAPTER 5

Back home

Midwifery has become part of my favorite aspect of the nursing profession. As a result, I was committed to work as a practicing midwife at my home school, Whittington Hospital. The students must witness 10 deliveries and deliver 10 under supervision. That was the procedure for every student who came in to train as a student midwife, whether or not they wanted to work in obstetrics. One of the functions of working in the midwifery department included taking care of mothers and babies after delivery, such as breast-feeding and general hygiene before and after handling babies. Working in all those areas was a good thing.

The mother and father were pleased to see and talk with the nurses who actually participated in delivering their baby. So, from delivery room we followed up, watched the progress of the baby, and assisted with feeding instructions and home care.

Now it is my time

After all that training and working in that capacity, it was my time to start a family. In the meantime I continued to work on my marriage with patience. One day it was up the other day it was down. I never knew what was going to take place on a daily basis, because my spouse had a real problem that needed attention. Yet, he refused counseling.

Now a baby is on the way. I worked to the end of the term because I felt well. On December 1960, my first daughter was born, weighed 7:11, beautiful, perfectly normal, thank God. While on maternity leave, I made full use of breastfeeding, even after I returned to work in six weeks. I breast fed for three months, at least, with no problem whatsoever. I employed a British nanny to care for her every day during my work schedule. The nanny was an elderly woman who did a marvelous job of caring for her, as though it was her own child.

In England, midwives were trained to deliver babies at home. However, it was mandatory to have your first child in hospital. Second pregnancy must be scheduled for home confinement, providing there was no complication during prenatal care. Consequently, I was looking forward to having my second child at home. After fifteen months, I was ready for home delivery with my second pregnancy. At that time, one had no idea what the baby's sex was until after delivery. To me, the surprise was good.

March 1962, my home was ready. Labor began and progressed rapidly. It was a little difficult, for when the midwife came I was too far advanced to have Demerol—pain medication, but I needed something to ease the pain so badly. It was unbearable and I was expected to push that baby out despite the horrible pain I was experiencing. With the midwife saying "push" and I insisted I could not because the pain was too intense, we had a tugging and warring going on between us. Eventually, I managed to give one push and there was another girl. She weighed 7lbs.4 ounces, healthy, beautiful and very hungry. I breast-fed her immediately, and continued for three months with no problem. After about three months I started her on formula.

Shortly after I began formula she developed bowel obstruction. It was called Intussusception. The only symptom was projectile vomiting after each formula. She was not able to retain the food and her bowel was not active. Doctors performed emergency, abdominal surgery to repair the problem. Fortunately, it was not necessary to cut and join the bowel, which we called "anastomosis." They were able to milk the bowel to repair the problem. As I watched my daughter, lying there with tube in her nostril, intravenous solution using the vein in her head, was a grieving moment for me.

The surgeon explained the outcome of the surgery: "The lower part of the bowel—the cecum was high. Whether the intussusception caused the high cecum or the high cecum caused the intussusception we could not tell, but fortunately we were able to correct the problem without cutting the bowel and joining them together." He explained. I was grateful. She healed quickly without any post-operative problem.

Ongoing domestic problem

Do you wonder why women tolerate abuse in their marriage? Mine was always, "Don't tell anybody." And so, I had to put on a pleasant face, acting as though life was great in our home. In addition, my spouse was always apologizing after the fact. He was always seeking forgiveness. Yet he refused to seek counseling with or without me.

On the street, as we walked home together, I dare not look to the right or to the left, or else trouble awaited me when we got home. I would have to give an account for something I didn't know about such as, "Why was this man looking at you?" "Where did you know him?"

Not realizing I had an admirer, I had no idea what to say.

He would say, "This man looked at you," or "Why did you say so and so during our conversation at the table?"

The situation was horrendous. Every time we were out, I had to be careful what to say or what not to say. The tension was high. Socially, there was no relaxation, no peace. It was constant nagging and if I were to answer, or try to give a reason, it would end up with physical damage to my body.

Despite this, we were getting ready to migrate to America at my sister's invitation. She arranged citizenship for my spouse and me even before we left England. We both looked forward to the move and I hoped things would change for the better as far as the marriage was concerned. I expected my third child and realized the move meant leaving one cold country to come to another. Nonetheless, we looked forward to the change.

A new move

August 1964, we migrated to the United States with our two daughters, and a third on the way. However, we packed up, left our house in care of a real estate broker who would sell it for us. That was not too difficult at the time. We left England and arrived in New York safely.

My sister prepared a welcome celebration for us. Old friends whom I hadn't seen for many years were among the welcome guests. This was a pleasant surprise, to be able to see and fellowship with old friends. It was very thoughtful of my sister to arrange such a gathering. She migrated to America soon after she graduated from her nursing education in England. As a supervisor on the evening shift, she was able to secure a job for me at Unity Hospital, her place of employment in Brooklyn, New York. She prepared an accommodation for us at her apartment which was very near to the hospital where she worked, and made an appointment for me to see the Nursing Director. Even though I was six months pregnant, the Director gave me permission to work for as long as I could. So I took her advice and worked to the last day before going into labor. Meanwhile, our citizenship was being handled by an attorney.

November 17, 1964. Labor began. My sister prepared me so as to free the nurses of that assignment when I arrived at the labor room. Sometimes working to the end of the term makes labor easy. That's how it was for me with each pregnancy. Contractions progressed rapidly and I readied myself for the hospital. My sister notified the supervisor to expect me.

Oops! My membranes ruptured (my water is broken). Now I have to be careful because baby number three can pop out very quickly. I resided close to the hospital and walked slowly as the baby was descending rapidly. Even getting in a car was seemingly dangerous at this point. I made it to the delivery room with the baby's head on the perineum, ready to be delivered. The supervisor met me downstairs at the lobby. Fully ready, I feared that I would deliver the baby in the elevator.

Therefore, I had a heavy task of tightening myself to keep the baby from coming in transit. Labor progressed rapidly. Here comes another healthy, beautiful, 8 lb. girl.

The joy continued, but verbal and physical abuse was part of the territory. Migrating to America did not stop the abuse. Again, my spouse was always sorry, crying and promising to change his behavior. Yet, he would not seek counseling, always saying, "we can work it out together."

Control of money

From the onset of the marriage, my spouse was in charge of handling the finances. I handed him my signed paychecks, and he was in total control of doing what was necessary for the household. He simply enjoyed handling the financial aspect of the marriage. That made him happy. He did the shopping, including clothing and personal items for me. Yet, his behavior remained the same. That is why I knew he had a mental problem and needed help, even though he refused counsel.

In 1965, we took the three children to Grenada to meet George's parents and family. We left them there while I completed the requirements for licensure from the State Education department in Albany. I met my father-in-law in Grenada who lived alone in a secluded place. George did not speak of it, but his father was obviously mentally ill. I don't know of his origin but he was a white man, and seemed deserted by the family. Nobody made mention of him, but George introduced me to him while standing outside and saying, "Daddy, this is my wife." I was not given the opportunity to shake his hand, and George did not go close to him, but stood afar off. I did not ask any question because it was obvious nobody in the family wanted to discuss him. He was quiet and seemed harmless. I had never been to that parish before, and didn't know the family. It had been many years since I left Grenada having spent my childhood years in another parish before leaving for Aruba.

After spending a week with the family, we returned to New York. I completed the task of preparing for licensure. It included high school test, comprehensive nursing, and eight weeks of psychiatric nursing at Manhattan State Psychiatric Hospital. All went well. I loved the experience, especially comprehensive nursing.

Scheduled surgery

In 1966, one morning I experienced a sudden sharp abdominal pain and called in sick. I visited my doctor who gave me an injection for pain. I felt better and reported for duty the following morning. One of the attending specialists, a cardiologist, met me along the corridor and we discussed what was happening with me. He suggested I do a gall bladder series.

I followed his instructions, consulted my personal physician, and the report revealed stones in the gall bladder. I consulted a surgeon who was on staff at the hospital. He scheduled surgery. George thought I should wait. Of course, money was not going to be coming in for two months. He was not looking forward to that, but my health was at stake.

I decided that another bout of severe pain was not what I wanted to experience. The surgeon scheduled surgery and I gave the report to my husband who suggested I wait for a while. That was a bad idea. The surgeon performed surgery and the results revealed a very serious problem. Many stones lodged in the common bile duct could have caused serious trouble for me. Consequently, it was a good decision to take care of it immediately. I healed very quickly, and returned to duty in about eight weeks. I kept the stones in a bottle for many years until I got rid of them.

In 1967, George and I went back to Grenada for the children. His sister took good care of them, but because of their surroundings they developed a terrible language problem. The strong undesirable words kept flowing from their mouths as a normal part of their vocabulary, especially with my second daughter. We came back to America and had much to accomplish with the children. One good thing, the same way they learned those foul language, they were able to unlearn quickly as they came back to America and got settled in school. At 2 years old, my third daughter didn't want to see me. Her aunt was her mother and that was understandable. She had no idea who I was. Eventually, she was no longer with her aunt in Grenada and had no choice in realizing I was her mother. Auntie came for a visit and at that time there was no doubt in her mind who was Mother. She could now differentiate between her mother and her aunt.

There was yet not one word uttered about Mr. Preudhomme, George's father, when we went back to Grenada for the children. I often wished I could ask about him, but I assumed that was a subject not to be discussed, especially with me. What an awful shame to be in a relationship where one is not free to discuss issues like these.

However, we were all together again learning to cope with life. There was a possibility of an addition to the family. In the beginning George suggested three children. I would like at least four, and stop whenever God puts in His order. It is good to watch children develop if the Lord has blessed you with the opportunity to do so. Two years after the children return from Grenada I was ready for another child.

1968. The fourth and last pregnancy. Because of the position and the weight I was carrying with that pregnancy, I was certain "that had to be a boy." I was large and heavy with no obvious problem. The time came at the end of nine months, I was anxious to have that baby boy spoiled by his sisters. I was in America and had not heard anything about doing a sonogram to determine the baby's sex. That was not in effect until years later. I worked throughout the pregnancy with no undue discomfort.

Labor began, and I got to the hospital on time. As labor progressed without delay, the nurses wheeled me into the labor room where my doctor awaited me. A few minutes later, the doctor and nurses shouted, "It's a girl!" So this was girl number four, beautiful, healthy, and weighed 9.6 lbs. They weighed heavier each time. Now the doctors are contemplating the possibility of pre-diabetic because of the weight of the baby. But they were not going to have another opportunity to determine that, because this was going to be my final pregnancy. And so it was.

Promotion on the job

Within two years of employment, the Director of Nurses summoned me to the office and offered me a supervisory position. That required months of orientation. Part of my orientation required me to work at the nurses' station and take charge of one of the medical units. There were some challenges in that the charge nurse was not too happy about this position. The next day she called in sick. That did not deter me at all. To make it worse, the unit clerk called in also.

The unit clerk is invaluable on the unit to help with the paper work and other clerical aspect of the department. However, as a result of my appointment, she called in sick. From this you get the picture of what was happening as a result of this promotion.

The supervisor came to the unit and was surprised I had not called her for assistance. I had no need to report any problems because God is a good God. He gave me peace despite the deceit. At that hospital, I catapulted the ladder of success from supervision to Assistant Director of Nursing Services, and Director of In-service Education. Despite the abuse at home I was able to hold on to a position at the institution. When God is for you no man can be against you. According to the Scripture, "No weapon that is formed against you shall prosper" (Isaiah 54:17).

CHAPTER 6

Higher Education

Knowing what was happening in my marriage one of the supervisors invited me to go to CUNY, one of the city universities of New York. I started a degree program at Brooklyn College and graduated with a Bachelor's Degree in sociology, with a minor in economics. I attended school in the evenings and concluded that this would keep me sane and busy. A number of women allow problems of this magnitude to dominate their lives and keep them from making progress in their everyday activities. As a result, they choose to indulge in alcohol, and end up as suicidal. Even though I did not know how to pray effectively, God protected me. Despite the circumstances, you can trust Him. The Scripture says, "Trust in the Lord, and do good so shall you dwell in the land and verily you shall be fed" (Psalm 37:3). The Lord asked us to trust Him.

A good education is an asset. It allows you to think soberly. Also, it helps you to focus on positive aspect of life, and enables you to move to new level in God. This will give you an opportunity to help those who are experiencing similar situations.

Terrorism in the college parking lot

Coming out from class one night accompanied by two other students and one of the teachers, I found two of my car tires slashed. Two of the individuals exclaimed, "This is vandalism!" That did not stop me from proceeding with my education. In fact, it made me strong even though I was going through turmoil in my life. When you find yourself in a tight spot, you don't have to turn to alcohol or drugs. You don't have to look at suicide as an option. God is too good to you. Simply accept Him as Lord of your life. He says in His Word, "I am in my Father, you are in me, and I am in you" (John 14:20). What an honor and a privilege to know that we are one in Christ Jesus. He sees and knows all that is taking place in our lives. During my ordeal, I didn't know how to communicate with God through His Word. The Bible was not part of my reading materials, but I realized God was attentive to me. He kept me alive when death was imminent. Oh, what a Mighty God He is.

Today, I can share of His marvelous encounter in my life. Because of that I would like every individual to receive Him as Lord of your life. When friends would forsake you and become tired in their relationship with you, God is ever so near. You don't have to go to the mountain to look for Him.

Many individuals are of the opinion they must take a trip to the mountain to find God. You don't have to go that far. You don't have to take a swim across the lake or seek Him in the most unlikely places. He lives within you. Get hold of the Bible and read His Word. You will find Him on every page of this great Book. In it you will find life and power to stand against the forces of evil. The Scripture says, "The word is quick and powerful, and sharper than any two-edged sword, piercing even to the dividing asunder of soul and spirit, and of the joints and marrow, and is a discerner of the thoughts and intents of the heart" (Hebrews 4:12). It's powerful.

For the Word that God speaks is alive and full of power. It is rich in nourishment for your body, soul, and mind. When I think of what I went through during my marriage, it is the mercy of God that kept me alive in the midst of the abuse. As I look back at all this, I can say with bold assurance, the Lord definitely had a special plan for me.

Regardless of what the devil throws in your paths, know that God is going to fulfill His plan for your life. And so, even though you are going through what seems to be unbearable, there is power in the Word of God. Take it as your daily bread. Apart from the Scriptures that the Lord has been giving me, I find comfort in the words of Jesus, "Let not your heart be troubled: you believe in God, believe also in me" (John 14:1). You can always turn the pages of St. John's Gospel and find words like, "Peace I leave with you, my peace I give unto you . . . let not your heart be troubled, neither let it be afraid" (John 14:27). This is comforting to me. In fact, for the last two years the Lord placed the Gospel of John in my spirit, and insisted I spend time in the Book of John. I realize He does not just want me to read but study that Book. As a result, I read and spend much time in the Gospel of John.

How much more can one take?

If while you are being physically abused you do your utmost to help your spouse by directing him to counsel, there is a time when you come to a crossroad and ask yourself, how much more can I take? My spouse refused counseling, repeatedly asked me to forgive him, and this was an ongoing request for which I complied liberally. This had no effect on the marriage. The only means of resolving this abusive situation was through counseling in the name of Jesus. Failing this, it was time to seek legal advice. After trying hard to defend my marriage, I came to the conclusion that in order to keep my sanity and live, I had to do something about this situation.

I consulted an attorney to work for me. The proceedings began and my spouse promised to change his behavior. I called my attorney and cancelled the divorce proceedings. That was just a figure of speech. He did not intend to change. I kept calling my attorney off and on. By this time I am certain he was disgusted with my constant calling and canceling the divorce proceedings. I, too, was certainly tired of the drilling game. It was so frustrating. However, I decided to give it another try, one more time. I continued to remain faithful with the financial arrangement with my signed check, and he was happy with that more than anything else. He also enjoyed preparing my uniforms when I worked 16-hour shift. Even though he was psychologically imbalance, I kept holding on because I realized that was something inherited as far as I could see. Consequently, I gave him the benefit of the doubt. If only he would consent to counsel, we could make a great life together, I thought.

During some of his temper tantrums, he would close the blinds so that the neighbors would not see what was happening in our home. He received a letter from his sister who wrote on behalf of his mother. The letter instructed him not to hurt me, a useless instruction. I was almost sure if he would seek counsel all would be well. But no matter what I said he would not take heed but continued his abusive treatment then asked for forgiveness.

One evening, while handing out his abusive treatment, my spouse held on to my blouse, twisted it with intent to damage my breasts, saying, "No one else will have you!" That was the kind of madness I had to tolerate on a regular basis. It was a sickness that drove him in an insane mood at his leisure. However, because of the impression he portrayed, no one would believe he was capable of such atrocious behavior.

Visit from his sister

George's sister visited from Grenada. She was disturbed about the situation in our home and the treatment her brother was delivering to me. One evening, she and I were having a quiet conversation in the bathroom. She was very embarrassed and admitted she would not be able to tolerate the kind of abuse her brother was delivering to me.

After a few minutes George knocked on the bathroom door, demanding that we come out. Fearing her brother, Sister Anna flushed the toilet to give the impression she was actually using the commode/toilet. She was the one who had written to him years prior on behalf of her mother concerning his treatment towards me. Personally she was witnessing the abuse and felt badly for me. Obviously, his family knew of his temperament. He had three sons by three different women, and later I found out that those women suffered tremendous abuse by him, such as kicking them at his pleasure. I did not know him nor about those relationships until after the marriage.

Put a stop to the madness

The buck stops here. Womanhood must be back in its place. One pay period I worked overtime and cashed the check to buy something personal for myself. I gave him all the money and I held back the overtime portion I needed for myself. War broke out in the home. I dare not cash my check. I must bring the signed check, and hand it to him. Well, I had been doing that for many years at the onset of our marriage, without malice. Now I must put an end to the madness and demand some kind of respect.

Enough is enough. He refused to accept the cash from me. I had no problem with that. I am a person of value, God's child. Now he refused to share some of the responsibilities in the home. I took the liberty, used my paycheck to fulfill the responsibility in the home. I paid all the bills as they came due, including the mortgage, without his support. I took full responsibility of caring for the home and the children with the money I had in my possession every pay period.

My spouse's love for money, his desperation to handle my wages and spend it as he sees fit, was no problem as far as I was concerned. I simply wanted to get something for my hair. For that I used only the extra money and gave him my regular salary. The fact that I was beginning to have some independence infuriated him even more. In fact, everything infuriated him without knowing what it was. Also, I had no idea why he demonstrated such an insanely jealous character even before the marriage.

Eventually, all that had to come to an end because no human being can tolerate this kind of insanity forever. I know there are many women out there who are going through this kind of abuse, but because of fear and insecurity they can't tell anybody, not even a counselor. I, too, could not tell anybody. I was fearful but my spouse asked me not to tell anybody. Talking to a counselor was out of the question since he refused to involve a counselor in the situation.

Child in the midst

My treatment became so overbearing I began to sleep in the children's room. On occasion, he came to the room and caused havoc by overthrowing my bed. I could remember my first daughter coming to my rescue.

"No daddy, don't." She cried.

She came between us on many occasions during periods of physical abuse.

That child witnessed so much of that behavior. She pleaded and begged,

"Daddy stop, don't hit Mummy."

At the age of about 11, she became heavily involved in the dispute to save my life. Even when the others were not aware what was going on because they were asleep, they all at some point became involved in the happenings. For example, my third daughter, Sonya, was sitting in the kitchen one day when her father was threatening and pushing me.

Sonya said," Daddy leave her alone."

"Do you see me hit her?" He asked, angrily.

"No, but you pushed her." Sonya replied.

He became so angry and annoyed with the child that she never attempted to defend me again. He made sure that her attitude toward me was no longer the same. He fixed it so that she could never utter another word. Her attitude towards me changed completely, from one of love to hate, just suddenly. Are you getting the picture?

Crying to get his way

With both hands on his head, my spouse is crying bitterly in the presence of his friends. "Things would never be the same unless she brings me the check." We had agreed to do this after marriage, and I was happy to do so, because it meant nothing to me. He liked to do the shopping and banking. I liked to know that I could work 8-16 hours and place the signed check in his hands. That was no problem to me. He was the one who refused the money one pay period because it was not in the form of a check.

Wickedness prevailed while using the children

The children not only became involved in the domestic slander at home, but their father removed them from school to attend the court hearing during the divorce proceedings. There was absolutely no reason for that. Despite his strong arm at home, he was very insecure and thought he could use the children as a front, to prove that the divorce was not warranted because of them. On the contrary, they had seen enough. Their minds were consumed with the tragedies that they faced daily.

My spouse poisoned the children's minds and made sure their affection would be towards him. He brainwashed them completely. I was advised to talk to the children so that they would know the truth. I felt this was going to be too confusing for them, with one parent saying this, the other parent saying another. This could be too confusing for young children. I knew Shelley, our first daughter, was old enough to remember how she got involved in the fights and pleaded for me on numerous occasions. She was 12 year old at the time of divorce, and that must have been a relief for her. For years, this child was in the midst of the dispute, and for one year got heavily involved by trying to protect me during physical attacks.

Whenever the evil rose up in him my spouse would take the car keys from me. I would have to find public transportation for work. I bought a new car which served me well for many years. I was able to do that while I had the privilege of handling my paycheck. He worked on Wall Street and used the train. He had no need for the car. He knew the car was important to me because of my work schedule, especially being on the evening shift. Taking the keys was his means of punishing me.

Hammer in his hand

One morning I was in the kitchen over the sink washing some dishes. My spouse took a hammer and directed it at me, saying what he would do if I were to fight for the house that we owned together. He was lashing out on the kitchen wall with the hammer saying, "This is the house you want? I'll break it up!"

Meanwhile, his means of control was to indulge in heavy witchcraft. He was so insecure and knew that in the natural he stood to lose. And so, he turned to the profession with which he was most familiar. In fact, witchcraft is still his means of control over the children. He insisted he must have the house. As a result, he threatened me every day. I submitted and agreed that he could have whatever he desired. Even then he was not satisfied. He continued to threaten me verbally. The divorce proceedings were bitter, almost inhumane happenings. He looked for pity and used the children at his pleasure jeopardizing their education.

While we were working and especially since I was making more money as a nurse in overtime, I suggested we invest in real estate. His reply was. "Let's put the money in the bank and watch it grow." In those days, investing in real estate was the best decision one could make. Any-one with a business sense invested in something substantial, instead of leaving money in the bank at that time. That was his way of thinking. He had to see and feel the money in his hands. It gave him a sense of power. He had to be able to look at the bank book and feel happy, as opposed to investing in a piece of property like real estate.

Attorneys' conversation

Because the divorce proceeding was strange, and because the attorneys both realized my spouse had a major problem, the two attorneys became friends. One day I had a call from my attorney:

"Why are you cohabiting with your husband?" He asked.

"He wouldn't leave me in peace." I replied. "He comes to the children's room where I sleep and pulls me off the bed." I said.

It is the most difficult thing filing for divorce while living in the same house with the abuser, especially if the divorce is contested. He had a good reason why the divorce should not take place because we were cohabiting. He made sure his attorney was aware of that so he had something substantial to hold on to as a reason to cancel the divorce.

We had left the house in London in the care of a real estate broker. I had no idea when they sold the house or what he did with the income from the transaction.

Therefore, I put a stop on our bank account in Brooklyn, New York. Neither he nor I could use the funds.

My family must not know what was going on in the marriage, and I tried to keep all this from them. Nonetheless, my youngest sister was getting ready to bless her baby. My spouse had no intention of going to the celebration. He had no specific reason. I attended the function. Later he came to my sister's home and demanded that I leave. He followed me around the house, even to the restroom and attempted to pull me out of the room. It was an embarrassing moment for me. Eventually he rushed out of the house with anger that could create an earthquake.

The next morning as I was about to leave for my home, I had a telephone conversation with our friends only to find out that I had no clothes. "What do you mean I have no clothes?" I asked.

Accompanied by my brother-in-law I left my sister's home, headed for my home, not knowing what to expect. The uncertainty was stressful to say the least. What I found when I arrived home was unthinkable and horrible. I proceeded to look into the closets. I opened one closet and found it empty. A second was empty, and there were no clothes in the house. I checked the basement. Every item of clothing was in the middle of the floor cut in pieces. Hats, shoes, pocket books, bags, fur coats and every imaginable thing were in pieces, a real mad man's work. The children were looking on pitifully, standing around my belongings in the basement.

My spouse and I did not exchange one word. Accompanied by my brother-in-law, I left the house and went back to my sister where I planned to stay for a few days while I shopped for new uniforms, clothing and personal items before going out to work. Meanwhile, I called the Nursing Director and informed her of my predicament. I needed a few days off. She was sympathetic and understanding and looked forward to my reporting for duty as soon as I could.

CHAPTER 7

Back on the job

I shopped for uniforms, shoes and other clothing that I would need immediately, and reported for duty. Inundated with phone calls from my spouse, the Nursing Director was accused of knowing where he could find me. However, she could not supply him with any information because she really didn't know where I was. He visited the hospital frequently hoping to see me, and insisted that the Director tell him where he could find me. She notified me that my husband had been calling and insisting that she divulge my where about to him. I apologized to her and explained what transpired at home at that time. Not the whole story.

My spouse continued to harass me on the job. He even insisted that the Director encourage me to go back home. However, because of the children, I must endure this horrible relationship.

I have been tolerating all this abuse from the onset of the marriage because of them. How long must I go on? I questioned myself. I refused to consult friends or family at this point. When I finally made the decision to run for my life, I did not seek the advice of my siblings. Even though my spouse was always of the opinion I couldn't do anything by myself, getting out of that brutal relationship was solely my decision.

Reconciliation

Could you believe it? I was home again. My spouse was going to change for good. Crying bitterly, asking for forgiveness as usual, he was sure we could work this out together. I reminded him about counseling one more time.

"I don't need counseling." He said.

"George, I'll go with you." I said.

"No, we can work this out without counseling." He replied.

There was no change, the abuse continued on a regular basis.

One morning, one of my co-workers and her husband visited unannounced. They came to see me and George directed them to the bedroom where I was resting after a physical encounter the previous night. He was nursing my black eye, and said to my friends, "this was an accident." He was quite good at nursing me back to health. Even though he insisted no one should know what was happening in the home and in the marriage, at times it was obvious to the public that things were not always what they appear to be. For example, God would have it that my co-worker visited me and witnessed an obvious black eye. Even the children's schoolteachers became aware of the problem when one of my daughters became ill, and vomited at school. Her teacher found out what was happening at home. I spoke to the teacher who said, she spoke to the child and let her know that she—the teacher—would not tolerate the kind of abuse her mother was experiencing.

You see, this daughter pondered everything in her heart without saying anything, resulting in illness. Eventually her teacher learned what the problem was and how it was affecting the child. So, just when I thought one child understood what was going on and got involved by trying to stop her father from seriously hurting me, there was another child who kept everything in her heart, said nothing, but carried the burden which caused her to suffer emotionally. As a result, her teacher observed keenly, found out that the domestic problem at home attributed to the emotional dilemma.

For fear of my life, I didn't dare take it to court. Nonetheless, I got the opportunity to report one incident to the police. They instructed me to go to family court. They could not intervene "unless it was a matter of life and death." They explained. In other words, somebody would have to die in the process before the police could do anything about the situation. But there is always a day of reckoning when everything must come to an end. I have been looking forward to the day when God would say, "Enough is enough."

One evening I came home very tired from a hard day at work. I went to the children's room, checked on them and prepared for bed myself. My spouse began to strip me and to search my underwear. I thought, "Enough is enough." For the first time in my adult life, I developed some no-nonsense strength, got hold of my slipper and hit him in his face. I thought he would kill me after that so I called the police. They came promptly and found both of us fairly calm and George seemingly was the one who was hurting at the time. After a short conversation they left. With no further ado we settled down for the night and slept comfortably.

What can you make of that? It seems that a man like that would do well to have a strong woman, a no-nonsense person from the onset of the marriage, who would demonstrate boldness. Such a woman would demand respect and, most likely, receive it.

Divorce is final

After a horrible contested divorce, taking the children from school to have them accompany him to court, the divorce was finalized and I have custody of the four children with visitation rights. The decision was that he paid child support of $45 a week for the four children. He was not required to pay alimony because I was self-sufficient.

Do you think the battle was over? He fought and bullied his attorney, and I agreed to let him have the house that he so desperately refused to give up. In addition, the divorce decree must not show him as the abuser. He must look good on those papers, and I must appear as the abuser. He has the house and I settled for $4500.00. I bought a second home and relocated to my new residence without the children. He insisted I must not have them.

"I'll kill them all." He said angrily.

I moved the children's furniture and some of their belongings, and his friends assisted me in moving. He later accused his friends of taking his wife from him. Now he has the opportunity to poison the children's minds, even though they witnessed all that transpired in the marriage. Wickedness prevailed and he used witchcraft to overpower the children. They are under complete control of his demons. He sold them to the devil from childhood. But God is patiently watching the situation. He will deliver them in His own time and season.

I attempted unsuccessfully to take the children to their new home. However, he agreed that I could have the last child because he could not handle the babysitting problem. I had registered her in a private school, 'Little Flower Montessori.' She was 2 ½ years old and was ready for school. George accused me of wasting money by enrolling her in that school, and that I should not spend that kind of money on her. I believed it was a good thing because she was bright, and ready for learning. She enjoyed the school and the teachers loved her.

One Saturday morning we were out shopping and met the other children with their father. She requested to go home with them. It was only fair, so I agreed to let her go. At that time she was happier to be with her sisters, and that was natural.

Peace was not to be in my territory

After the divorce, peace was not to be in my house. Coming from church on Sundays, I looked in my rearview mirror and there was George following me. This continued every Sunday after the divorce, until he came out of the car and tried to befriend me.

This time it was too late. The divorce was final. I had much more than I could take. He would be crying over my grave using his password, "I am sorry." After parking my car in the garage, I walked up to my front door. He followed me to the door.

"Connie, let's get married again." He said. (Connie is my home name for Constance).

"Get it into your head we are divorced." I replied.

Well, that was too much for him to take. Furious, he rushed down the stairs and vowed: "You will never be happy with another man!" He said. I had never beheld such anger. After all the suffering, verbal and physical abuse, he expected a reunion. We have been having many reunions with no change. I would be out of my mind to go back to that hellish domain.

The witchcraft became worse than ever, but I am still alive. Thank God. You think you are divorced so you are free from the demonic attacks. Let me tell you, it's just beginning. From an abusive spouse who wants to get back into my life, he is really saying, this time I will fix you for good. 'Come back home to die.' He would not accept the separation, yet refused psychological help or some form of counseling. It's a tragedy. He had said that unless I bring the check to him life would never be the same. Now, in addition to his psychological problems, he couldn't deal with the fact that he was not handling those checks. I didn't consider it my money while we were together. To me, it was a normal thing to do—sign and give him the check every fortnight was no threat to me.

Just imagine; the unjust punishment and continued brutality he called life. "Life would never be the same." He said. Of course, that life could never be the same. He has the house that he fought for, yet unhappy. He could not handle the fact that I bought another home. He was always of the opinion that, because he handled all the finances, I was incapable of doing anything on my own. Therefore, buying a home and managing without him was somewhat of a shock to his ego. I tolerated all the abuse because it was not my desire to separate, especially having children who loved both parents. It's a tragedy, but life has to go on despite the devil's intervention. I am alive today to testify of the goodness of God. He keeps my mind from becoming corroded with the evil that's trying to block my paths.

1978 Jobless

After 14 years of service, the hospital became defunct; a time when all the small hospitals were struggling to stay alive in New York. The hospital management advised the staff to go to the unemployment office to register for food stamps. That was an experience in itself. Shortly after that I received a call from one of the administrators offering me a position at another small hospital. It seemed senseless accepting that position when the hospital management was struggling to keep it alive. It was also on the list for shutting down.

However, I decided to accept the position of Director of Nursing Services. Even though I could not save the hospital, I worked hard, and with the co-operation of the staff, Joint Commission of Accredited Hospital (JCAH) came in a few weeks after my appointment, to carry out their inspection. They were pleased and gave us an excellent evaluation. I enjoyed one year's experience before that hospital ceased to function. Before that, I had to dismiss the per diem staff. Even though I hired them for temporary work they couldn't understand why I was terminating them. To avoid chaos I had to be discreet and couldn't tell them the hospital was being closed. I terminated one at a time so that the staff would keep calm while patients were being cared for before transferring them to various institutions, or discharging them to their own homes.

Finally, the transition went on smoothly, all patients were discharged, and the nurses realized they had to seek employment elsewhere. One of my daughters was part of the per diem staff. Other jobs became available and I accepted private duty assignments for a while until I received another call from a previous co-worker who was being elevated, and offered me her position in administration. That was another hospital trying to survive in the city. Insisted on staying employed, as long as God gave me the opportunity, I was not refusing any opportunity that came my way. Therefore, between private duty and short-term positions, I accepted the post.

Demonstration of anger increased

I bought another property, a small apartment building. After my spouse became aware of that, he tried every trick of the trade to destroy me. He must get some money from me. He took me to court again. What a trial. Money was driving him more insane. It was money from the beginning, and it is going to be money that drives him to his grave. Jealousy, false accusation, verbal abuse, and physical abuse then one day per week he returns to normal. What a life!

Family Wedding

Years later, our first two daughters were married, one in Barbados the other in New York City, 1986 and 1992 respectively. Since then their father forbade the other two children to have me at their wedding. He is married to the neighbor's daughter, a young divorcee with no children. Even then, he is still unhappy. I have no idea why, but he follows me wherever I go and tries to exact money from me by taking me to court at his pleasure. I have no idea what he has done with the money from the sale of the property in London, and from other bank accounts. Also, he fought for the house we bought together, yet he is not satisfied with his life, because he will not seek God. Instead, he works with the devil.

The highly contested divorce was over. He has a young wife, yet he will not leave me in peace. I don't understand his problem. The new marriage should be a happy one for him. Yet, he is so focused on what monies he could extract from me. He tries every wicked device, while I hold on to God, my Creator.

CHAPTER 8

A day in prison

Two police officers are at my door. "We have a warrant for your arrest," they said.

"What have I done?" I enquired. I invited them inside, and they were obviously surprised by what was taking place. They seemed confused themselves.

"Your husband has accused you of owing him money." They replied. "You are coming with us, but we are not going to put handcuff on you."

I appreciated that. The officers seemed particularly sympathetic. It was obvious this was very strange, and they demonstrated this in their attitude. They spent a few minutes with me while I got myself together and I walked out with them to their car. They took me into the courtroom.

It was late in the afternoon. I sat in the courtroom for about 15 minutes, very strange atmosphere. No one spoke to me. There was no hearing and George was not in court. Obviously his witches were assigned to the job, and he was confident they would work well for him. Meanwhile, a car was waiting to take me to jail at Riker's Island in New York.

I rode with three young people who bombarded me with questions. "Why are you going to jail?" We deserve jail, but what have you done?" They asked.

They were so sympathetic and insistent; I broke down and gave them an answer. "My x-husband is sending me to jail, accusing me of owing him money." I said.

Arrived at my destination

I arrived at Riker's Island. They fingerprinted me and gave me permission to make one phone call.

"Lucille, I am at Riker's Island. George ordered me here. He accused me of owing him money. My bail is $500.00, can you help?" I inquired.

"Yes, I'll talk to someone and we'll be there." She replied.

One of the church members put up the bail and came with Sister Lucille to get me. We left the prison area at 1 o'clock that night. The member who put up the bail said, "This is very strange. As long as you are a home owner you could take care of your own bail right there in the court." She couldn't understand the mystery. Even the police who brought me to court were confused about this situation. Obviously, that was a set-up by my spouse and his witches, not strange to me. This is whom I have been sleeping with for thirteen years. Mind you, this court proceeding is happening a few years after the divorce. I refused to get back together with him and so he vowed to destroy my peace. He lived and operated in heavy witchcraft during the divorce proceedings, after the divorce and even now. The children cannot think for themselves, even today. Their minds are ruined by their father's horrifying occupation. That's where his money goes, in the witches' pockets, and he expects me to supply the money for his habit. However, God is my Father and knows all things. He will straighten the matter in His time.

This backfired, it made me strong

I want to reiterate that the court ordered him to pay $45 in child support. He will do anything to avoid paying a mere $45 for four children. Instead, he dared me to take the children, and threatened to kill them all if I were to touch them. He is using this opportunity to extract money from me. He is going to court to claim child support from me because there is a new law in effect. This law demands that the woman is also responsible for paying child support. Now he is in his glory. Instead of paying $45 for child support, he forcefully kept them and used the opportunity to harass me for money.

After the jail experience, he was able to get one payment from me through the court. How-ever, that experience gave me some determination to put him in his rightful place. I refused to work on staff, and consented to work part time/per diem where I could schedule my own hours. What of his marriage to this young woman? It often baffles me. If she is real, what is she thinking? Does she know what he is doing? I wonder. In fact, knowing him, she dare not say a word. She will have her share of abuse. In fact, she is probably more daring than I. A young woman with stamina might be able to use some authority and demand respect, if she is not under his spell. In fact, she is probably having her share of confusion as he constantly seeks her forgiveness. His plea is always so tender, he melts like butter, so you have no choice but to say, "I forgive you," until tomorrow or the following day when he begins to act in a frightful manner.

Taking a break

1985-1986 I sold my properties and spent six months in Grenada, my home town, where I was able to follow through on my missionary work. I enjoyed working in the mission field, for there lays my heart. After six months I returned to New York and stayed in Bronx, New York, at the invitation of a family friend. I applied to

Our Lady of Mercy Medical Center for a part-time position and worked as needed. I relocated back to Brooklyn, New York, but kept my employment at the Bronx hospital working in obstetrics—maternity department.

Surprise call

One morning I was on duty when a call came from payroll department, asking to speak to me. I picked up the telephone to the sound of:

"Mrs. Preudhomme."

"Yes." I answered.

"I just want to let you know that your husband is garnishing your pay." They said.

"Are you serious?" I asked.

"Yes." They replied.

"Thank you very much." I said.

To iterate, the divorce proceedings ended since November 1972 and this is 1986. I refused to get back into a relationship with him so he vowed I must perish. Harassing me for money is part of his scheme, even in the 1990's. On the contrary, he defrauded me of monies from the sale of the house in England, and monies for which I worked so hard and handed him during the 13 years of marriage. Yet, his covetousness for money has added to his insanity.

CHAPTER 9

Missionary endeavor

I began my missionary journey on the streets of New York, preaching the Gospel, feeding the homeless in the Bowery Mission and on the streets, before traveling abroad to the mission field. After preaching on the streets of New York, and the Caribbean Islands including Trinidad, and Tobago, Grenada, St. Vincent, with my church family, the Lord directed me on a personal journey to my hometown, Grenada.

Therefore, in 1983 I began my personal journey starting in Grenada, and continued on to Trinidad and Tobago, St. Vincent and the Grenadines. Returning to New York, I continued street mission throughout the Borough of Brooklyn and Manhattan before traveling to the nation. In 1986, I accompanied a church group to Israel and Rome.

In 1988 I accompanied another church group on a world tour. That trip took me to India, China, Asia, Philippines and Hong Kong. We ministered in a home for retarded children in Asia, also in a church service in the Philippines. After a church service in India, my roommate and I had the pleasure of ministering on the streets of India. It was quite interesting even though we couldn't speak the language. I came back home to Calvary Pentecostal Church in Ashland, Virginia, and testified of the goodness of Jesus Christ before returning to New York.

In 1993, street ministry was high on my list of priorities, including preaching and ministering on the streets of Brooklyn. Those who could not get out of their apartments, we took the gospel directly to their homes. After moving from Bronx, N.Y., ministering on the streets of Brooklyn was a regular occurrence; sometimes alone and at times accompanied by another individual. Nonetheless, obstacles always presented themselves with the hope of stealing my joy.

June 1995, I planned a mission trip to Grenada. Amazingly, a man knocked on the door of my apartment in Brooklyn and handed me a subpoena to appear in court. I contemplated on what I should do. I had already planned the mission and was looking forward to spending some time with my mother. During my mission trips I had not been spending time with her, but this year I intended to stay and care for her as a priority.

Surprisingly, George is taking me to court again, 23 years after the divorce. Madness! "Should I cancel my mission trip?" I asked myself. One of my missionary partners encouraged me and said, "Don't cancel your mission, go home and take care of your mother, and don't hire an attorney." That sounded good to me. With trust and confidence that God will move on my behalf, I went to Grenada and started the mission right there in my mother's home.

God is awesome. The Scripture says: "Trust in the Lord with all your heart, and lean not unto your own understanding. In all your ways acknowledge him, and he shall direct your paths" (Proverbs 3: 5-6). I am going to take God at His Word, and believe He will fight my battle. Mother was in her 70's working hard at gardening around the house. That became her specialty. Since I have been bypassing her on each mission trip, I needed to make a change. I waited on her and refused to think about the court proceedings in New York. Every night I looked up to the heavens, the moon shining, as though I could touch the skies. The atmosphere was suitable for speaking to the Lord right there. I pressed in and sought Almighty God as He only can put every witchcraft spirit to flight.

To reiterate, the divorce proceedings ended in 1972. George is suing me for monies he owes me. So rather than seeking intervention of an attorney, I chose a better deal, a mission trip to Grenada, where God would intervene for me even while I was on His business. Looking after my mother who lived alone was part of His business. In addition to taking care of Mother, I checked the neighbor's blood pressure regularly and ministered to individuals in the neighborhood and other parishes. I prepared to return to New York believing God to work a miracle in the court.

After two weeks, I came back home to New York with a sense of knowing God was at work in my life and my situation. When you include Him in your business, victory is certain. After that trip I could testify of the goodness of God. All He requires is your faithfulness. Looking up to heaven in the moonlit night, I did a prayer walk every night around the house, while making my plea to Almighty God; then returned to New York to attend the court proceedings. God is an awesome God. There is benefit in serving Him.

Let me tell you, there is victory in serving God faithfully. No evil spirit can surpass God's intervention when you are serving Him. For the Scripture says, "God is a Spirit: and they that worship him must worship him in spirit and in truth" (John 4:24). It is having sweet fellowship with the Father, in the name of the Lord Jesus. Meditate on His Word, fulfill the mission, preach the Gospel. "Pray without ceasing" (1 Thessalonians 5:17). "Praying with all prayer and supplication in the Spirit . . ." (Ephesians 6:18). This is not to be done occasionally, but continuously, because the enemy is persistent.

Finally, this is it—God is in charge

I returned from Grenada just on time to answer my subpoena. I had a wonderful mission. Now God was ready to fight my battle. I entered the court room without an attorney. George did not have an attorney. God was faithful to give me the victory I deserve in the court's hearing. It did not take the judge five minutes to see the evil before his eyes. As a result, he made a just decision. He did not even require me to speak in the courtroom. All I managed to say as I interrupted the judge was, "Your honor, he is remarried and has a home in Albany with his new wife." "I don't need you to speak." The judge said.

However, I was happy to be able to get that quick word in his hearing. I could see that he was blessed with tremendous wisdom, and insight, and could see the tricks afar off. He saw no reason for that useless tactic. George left the courtroom burning with vengeance and a crushed ego, to poison the children's minds even more. He certainly succeeded in poising their minds. He gave them a good dose of his medicine.

This is an example of the importance of taking your eyes off your circumstances, do God's business, and He will take care of yours. God had intervened in the court room. Even though the judge was experienced and blessed with wisdom, I knew God was at work. I want to say to every-one reading this book, it is extremely important to seek God in everything you do. Keep your eyes off your problems and place them on Jesus Christ. He will deliver you in due season. He simply wants you to believe and trust Him. He shed His blood on the cross for you. He suffered much but He was victorious when He said, while on the cross, "It is finished" (John 19:30). For example, the devil tried everything to stop Him, but The Father made sure His mission was accomplished.

I don't know what George told the children, but all communication with them came to a halt. I can tell you, he did a work on them and on their minds. I must not seek them; they must not have me at their weddings. Here is how it worked: I called Lisa, my last daughter, and during our conversation I began to talk to her about the goodness of the Lord Jesus, and the importance of staying close to Him. Here is her response. "Mummy you need to hear yourself." She exploded. That took care of the need to get rid of me, so I would not be around for her wedding. I was not invited, but I was aware of the wedding plans.

Here is how Sonya handled her wedding plans. During our communication she said, "Mom, I don't want to hear anything about God, the God you say will punish Daddy. This God you're telling me about? I don't want to hear anything." This is the same child who tried to defend me and accused her father of hurting me many years ago. He fixed them real good, but I know God is not asleep. He will deliver them in His own time.

At times, I reflect on the trip to the jail and on the police officers who came and arrested me. I reflect on the armored car and the young women in that car with whom I travelled, and wondered how this could have happened in the manner in which it did. I could only mutter to myself, "Oh, what evil!"

I would like every reader of this book to know that God is stronger than the devil. He will deliver you if you stay in His presence and trust Him. Stay in the Word, and spend time meditating on what you have read, on a daily basis.

During my former years I did not know how to pray effectively. A sister introduced me to the Bible while I was in the Catholic Church. As I read it daily, it began to nourish my mind and soul with the Word of God. I began to understand what it meant to have fellowship with the Lord Jesus. Now, this is my nourishment before exiting my bedroom on mornings. It is rich information for every situation in our life. Neglecting it is depriving ourselves of the excellent teachings of Jesus Christ, and the deliverance that God intends for us. When I got hold of it, there was something precious about what transpired between God and me. What fellowship divine. There is no substitute for the Word of God. This is the reason I am alive today even though the devil is trying relentlessly to take me out of this world. God is merciful. His love is past understanding.

I continued mission work to the nation, especially in the Caribbean Islands until I retired in 1996, then sporadically until 2000 when I made what I thought was my final mission. A sister from Bolivia, South America asked me to join a group of pastors on a mission to her home town to do outdoor ministry in various parts of the country. I was assigned to preach for a week in seven different areas of the country. My interpreter was a Jewish brother residing in Bolivia.

I had never done such extensive preaching before, but it paid off well. It was a learning experience for me, and my Spanish lessons paid off. Each area was a different experience. That was one of my best trips as far as outdoor preaching was concerned. Most of my missionary journeys included outdoor preaching. However, Bolivia was a Spanish country and I had to move from one area to another each night not knowing what to expect.

One of the pastors, an American living in Bolivia, asked me to teach on missions. He had many young people who were interested in missions, so I accepted the invitation hoping one of the sisters in that ministry would assist me in my Spanish endeavor. One morning one of the sisters picked me up and took me to the church. I mixed English and Spanish together and we had a great time with that combination. The pastor did not attend the session. He left me to fend for myself with his members. The young ladies were the best. The pastor said they loved me.

Mission continued at home

I usually enjoyed camp meeting in Ashland, Virginia helping in the kitchen, or wherever I could. They usually got hold of me for an assignment in the kitchen. I became acquainted with Calvary Tabernacle while staying in the Bronx. It was an asset to become acquainted with that ministry. In 2003 I accompanied them on another trip to Israel and Egypt. After a week or two at the camp I returned to New York ready to function in my usual capacity at the hospital. That was the good thing about working part time. I was free to work for God whenever the opportunity presents itself.

Life-style change

Being on the mission field and seeking a higher education kept me busy. There was no time to worry about the evil that was coming against me. God is faithful and I am confident He will see me through this terrible ordeal. His power surpasses every wicked device that comes your way. If the Lord gives you an assignment or a vision, be obedient and stay with it. In the interim, He will fight your battle.

The Lord had commanded me to write a book, and to get back to my music, playing the piano. After some confirmation by my Bible school professors I began to write the book. It began with one of the professors at New York School of the Bible in New York City who commented on my writing in class. I had written an essay describing a man for whom the police was seeking.

The professor asked, "Mary, have you ever thought of writing for your local newspaper?"

"No." I replied. I pondered this in my heart for years, as I attended this particular Bible School from 1983-1986.

After many years hence, my professor of the doctoral program in Theology asked, "Mary, have you ever thought of writing a book? You could write your first book then a couple of sequels." The Lord had already asked me to write a book, supporting everything with Scripture. My dissertation for the doctorate was mainly on missions, so I wrote my first book entitled, "Branded for Missions," published by Author House in October 2005. In that book, I talked about my traveling experiences and my missionary journeys throughout the nation. It revealed some of the personal things that happened as I ventured on God's call for my life. It is important to get out there and minister to the hurting souls, especially those who are lost and do not know the Lord. This is much more important than staying home and being bombarded with personal issues that get you nowhere, instead, leave you with a lot of pain and anguish. As a result, I chose the mission field. What a journey!

The ensuing years I went back to England where I had my nursing education, and ministered on the streets of London. I accompanied a pastor to Jamaica, a place ripe for missions. In 2003 I made my second trip to Israel. On the mission to the Caribbean Islands, I had such compassion for the children, especially those in St. Vincent. I came back from the Island with a desire to shop for the children in that area. I sent a small barrel with clothing and personal items for the children in that village. Those children did not attend that church where I was located, but they came everyday to commune with me. I looked at them and noticed they needed some clothes and personal items. As a result, I shopped accordingly.

When the barrel arrived the church family notified and distributed the gifts to the children in the community. Those who did not receive a gift cried bitterly. I felt such compassion for those children and wished I could continue to send gifts for them. Nonetheless, that was somewhat strenuous for me, as I was alone and had no help.

From the onset of my mission to Grenada, shipping barrels with food and personal items were part of the project. The sisters who accompanied me contributed heavily to that mission. Also, I served hot foods to the Nursing Home clients in Grenada with the help of the people in the community. Also, I cooked and shared food to the homeless in Trinidad.

In addition, I served the children on the Island of Carriacou-Grenada. I felt such compassion for those children also. Yes, children have been the target of my mission. They always had a place in my heart, until the Lord opened a door to the prison ministry in Grenada where young men resided. It was good to preach the Word of God and encourage them to hold on to Jesus Christ who can change their lives. The good thing was, they were very receptive to the Gospel. They became part of my ministry whenever I visited Grenada.

Back to America, and back to work, hoping for another chance to take a flight to Grenada or any part of the Caribbean Islands. With no definite plan ahead, I got myself ready by getting little nuggets and gifts, because there is always a need for these things on the mission. Someone always expects me to bring a gift, whether it is a pair of socks, a pair of shoes, a notebook, pencil or pen. Clothing is always a necessity. I cannot over emphasize this. The time came for me to move again. I was never sure what direction the mission was going to take, but was always hoping for a tremendous move of God.

The Lord opened a new door in Grenada that enabled me to visit another nursing home, including a retarded children's residence in the same area. That was an additional assignment and I enjoyed every moment of it. Just to be able to care for those clients was a tremendous opportunity for those who were in charge of them. I was able to minister to them about Jesus Christ. Also, I used my nursing skills to check their blood pressure and give some advice regarding proper nutrition, especially for those whose blood pressure was elevated to an abnormal level. Also, a sister and I went to Trinidad on a mission and held a vocation bible school in one of the parishes on the Island. The results were tremendous. Children came by bus with much enthusiasm ready to participate in the sessions. That was one week and we were happy with the outcome.

We went to a remote area and did a health fare by checking blood pressures. The sister who was also a nurse, lectured, and I checked their blood pressure. An individual's blood pressure was extremely high and was difficult to get a clinic appointment without the visiting nurse's approval. We gave her garlic and had her sit for a while before checking her blood pressure again. That did not help a great deal. Nonetheless, we left with the hope she would adhere to the diet instructions we provided her.

Those mission trips gave me a reason to live, to be able to help people in whatever way I could. That was how I managed to survive the brutality that still continues after a bitter divorce. Mission was the best thing that could happen to me. I used the money that was in my possession to travel to the nations with the intention of helping people. Also, to encourage those who might be experiencing trials, and to encourage them that they, too, don't have to give up on life. There is much to be done in the kingdom. It is a good thing to take your eyes off the problems and look to Jesus. He is the only one able to keep you from falling. The Scripture tells us, "It is better to trust in the Lord than to put confidence in man" (Psalm 118:8). Sometimes even your loved ones may let you down. Here is a message from the Psalm penned by King David, "When my father and my mother forsake me, then the LORD will take me up" (Psalm 27:10). This is good consolation. You can encourage yourself with the Word of God. Though everything around you may seem foreign, you must take hold of God's Word. He will never leave you nor forsake you.

Everything else may change, but the Scripture says, "Jesus Christ is the same yesterday, and today, and forever" (Hebrews 13:8). In this time and season and even in your personal life, the battle is raging. According to the Scripture, we are engaged in a real battle against the enemy, and cannot afford to walk without our spiritual armor. Here is what the Scripture says:

> Finally my brethren, be strong in the Lord, and in the power of his might. Put on the whole armor of God that you may be able to stand against the cunning devices of the devil. For we wrestle not against flesh and blood, but against principalities, against powers, against the rulers of the darkness of this world, against spiritual wickedness in high places. Wherefore take unto you the whole armor of God that you may be able to withstand in the evil day, and having overcome all, to stand. Stand therefore, having your loins girded with truth, and having on the breastplate of righteousness; And your feet shod with the preparation of the gospel of peace; Above all, taking the shield of faith, wherewith you shall be able to quench all the fiery darts of the wicked. And take the helmet of salvation, and the sword of the Spirit, which is the word of God.
>
> —Ephesians 6: 10-17

Consequently, don't expect a smooth ride in your walk with God. Satan's plan is to destroy you, and he often uses your negative emotions toward that end. However, you win the battle by choosing to be anchored in God's love and faithfulness. Each time you choose to appropriate His truth to your circumstances, you are closer to winning the war. Satan's influence is diminished and, finally, you see him retreat. Let me tell you, it's a fight! The only way to accomplish the victory is staying close to Jesus Christ. Get in the Word of God. Use the Word to fight the devil and his cohorts. You can only succeed in the name of Jesus.

Today, there are multitudes of women suffering and they continue to be bombarded by the adversary. They feel completely lost because they are not acquainted with Jesus Christ, and for the most part refuse to make Him Lord of their life. When I didn't see Jesus as the most important person in my life, I made wrong decisions, walked in the imagination of my heart, and learned many hard lessons as a result.

Speaking from experience, I can say with a bold assurance that if you attempt to help someone, as opposed to meditating on your own sorrow, it will help you to get out of your lethargy. Then you will begin to feel relieved, and your spirit will have the freedom to praise God and give Him worship that He rightly deserves. You will definitely notice the change as you fellowship with Jesus.

Just imagine what I went through before I became acquainted with Jesus in His glory, and as my personal friend and Savior. I love Him and can testify of His goodness. As a child, I was brought up in church. Going to church every Sunday morning was mandatory, but I did not know Jesus as my Lord and Savior. One cannot know Him apart from reading His Word—the Bible. Knowing Him today is an asset in my life. He fights my battle and wins every time. Wonderful Jesus!

CHAPTER 10

Your own backyard

In 1999 my mother became ill in Grenada following a stroke, and was hospitalized at St. George's. My sister and I left America to nurse her at the hospital. The doctors asked that her children come because "she was not expected to live." My sister went home from Detroit and nursed Mother back to health. I followed before she returned to Detroit. We are three nurses in the family, all trained in England, as I mentioned previously. Here we were able to use that skill to care for Mother, and to see improvements before going back home. I spent some time with Mother until she was better. Surprised at her progress, the doctors discharged her. We left the hospital by ambulance, and I wouldn't want to describe the journey, for the roads were horrible and it seemed the driver had no mercy. We managed to get Mother to bed with no trauma. Thank God for that. Listen to me, when the doctors have given up on you, adequate nursing care will defy the medical report. Although it was not easy I continued to care for Mother at home. Apart from the medical problems, she had many social issues she needed to deal with. One serious problem was anger and un-forgiveness, as I explained in my first book.

Meanwhile, I interviewed a number of people to find a trustworthy person with whom I could leave Mother, before going back to New York. Finding a capable person was like finding a needle in a haystack. I found a young woman, and the way she treated Mother in my presence was atrocious. Could you imagine leaving Mother in the hands of that woman? If she could treat her so horribly in my presence, as soon as I turned my back Mother would be in total disaster. I continued the search for a person of integrity and patience.

Getting ready to leave

Finally I hired a young woman, a Christian, to care for her. My sister, Rhoda who lived in Michigan at the time, handled the financial aspect of caring for her. She had built a new home on the estate so that Mother could enjoy the comfort of that home. Even though I was assigned to care for her before returning to New York, there was always an open door for other missionary endeavor. And I never travel without preparing my mind for the possibility of an assignment.

Before leaving New York, I had settled in my spirit that I was going to have a revival service in the community center in that district. So, I made and printed some flyers with particular dates, hoping that the center would be available on those days. When I arrived in Grenada, I contacted the person in charge of the community center. He assured me, fortunately, nothing was going on at the center and those dates were perfect. The evenings were Sunday, Monday and Tuesday. I distributed the flyers and the services began with good attendance mostly from the neighborhood who requested prayer for various issues. We prayed, and ministered to them and the results were tremendous. They left feeling wonderfully blessed by God. I had invited a minister, a Grenadian living in Trinidad, to assist me in the ministry. He came willingly and was a great blessing to me.

When I look back at that endeavor I must have been quite daring and bold to set up a service, not knowing anything about the community's function. It just shows that once you are willing to proceed on kingdom business God will move with you. Take one step and you will find yourself simply moving in Him and with Him by faith. This means, even though you don't see an opening you can believe without a doubt that God will make a way for you to accomplish your goal. So there is always something you can do in your own backyard, and it is quite rewarding.

Before proceeding further, let me give you a definition of missions. We usually talk much about missions, but I think if the Church is aware of the blessings that could result from getting involved in missions, it will not hesitate to participate even starting at home base. I find a clear definition in Webster's Dictionary.

Mission defined

Webster's Dictionary defines mission as going out to reach those who are lost, to deliver those in captivity, physically, spiritually and mentally. It is the sending out of a group authorized to perform special service in the community. Specifically, mission is the sending out of persons by a religious organization to preach, teach, and convert the lost locally, and in foreign lands. It's to help those who are in need, and to bring about conversion in a district without a church of its own. I talked much about missions in my first book, but because this story is about my life, missionary work was part of my life's endeavor. Instead of worrying about the fiery darts that were coming at me, I occupied myself with kingdom business. So, there is always something with which you could occupy yourself instead of giving up on life.

The Bible says in the book of Matthew, "Go therefore, and teach all nations, baptizing them in the name of the Father, and of the Son, and of the Holy Ghost" (Matthew 28:19). His name is Jesus. This is the Great Commission. The Great Commission is an obligation to reach the lost at any cost. The way to accomplish this is through the preaching of the Gospel. It includes sharing and testifying about the Lord Jesus, His death, burial and resurrection. In today's world, we face tremendous problems, including the breakdown of the traditional family, the increased complexity of modern living, violence between the nations, and terrorism, even in the schools.

However, we need not despair. By the grace of God, it is precisely because of these problems the church has tremendous opportunities to share the Gospel, the Good News. Jesus came to set the captives free from the bondage of sin and corruption. This message is critical in this end time as people are becoming more and more perplexed about world situations, and are wondering when this will end. The problems are before us. Now what is the solution? This is no time to be out of touch with the needs of people, no time to invite needy people to church only if they accept the church's doctrine. To evangelize effectively, we must meet people where they are, not where we think they ought to be. One way to do this is to determine where they are and set target as to how we can reach them.

The possibilities for effective outreach are limitless, as the problems people face in this troubled world are immeasurable. Jesus commanded outreach ministry, and eventually this began due to persecution. It was limited ethnically at first, before the doors opened to all peoples. It flourished under adversity and decreased in prosperity. In other words, whenever there is a tragedy or a disaster, people turn to God. As soon as they are settled, rebuild their homes and communities, they begin to neglect the Gospel and behave as though they are responsible for rebuilding their own lives. God is left out of the picture entirely.

Neglected for a time, outreach ministry was discouraged until finally the doors opened for future progress. Since the church has moving orders to "Go into all the world and make disciples," and each local congregation has a part to play in obeying that order, the success of missions at all levels is of utmost importance. One can accomplish this by having a specific purpose, one of which is the conversion of the lost.

Since this is about my life and how I managed to stay alive, I love to share much about what kept me busy and how you, too, can use this as a tremendous benefit to help others and not focus on your own misgivings. Even while you are working in the kingdom of God you would sometimes feel like giving up because of the trials and persecution that face you on the journey. Here is an example of one of the Bible characters who were called by God, even in the midst of his rebellion. A perfect example of a missionary, his name was Saul. He persecuted the church of Jesus Christ, and was of the opinion he was working for God. God got hold of him in the midst of his rebellion against the church. On his way to Damascus in pursuit of his mission to persecute God's people, The Lord Jesus knocked him off his beast and immediately he became blind. He beheld a light from heaven and heard a voice saying unto him, "Saul, Saul, why do you persecute me?"

He responded with a question, "Who are you Lord?"

The Lord answered, "I am Jesus whom you are persecuting. It is hard for you to kick against the pricks" (Acts 9:4-5).

Trembling and astonished, Saul said: "What will you have me to do, Lord?" v.6

Jesus answered, "Arise and go into the city, and it shall be told you what you must do." v.6

Saul found the answer while on his knees, received his sight, filled with the Holy Spirit, and was never, ever the same again. He is now using the name Paul, on his way to becoming a great apostle with a dynamic mission to serve The Lord Jesus. Now he is being persecuted for the Word of God. He experienced much suffering in the ministry and insisted that nothing could stop him from serving the Christ whom he met on the Damascus road. Sometimes this is the only way one will obey and believe God, by having a harsh encounter with Jesus Christ in the midst of doing our own business. Paul is now on his way to suffer for the cause of Christ, his Redeemer and Lord. After he was delivered and filled with the Holy Spirit, Paul began to preach right there in the Synagogue at Damascus before going to Jerusalem. Everyone was amazed at this changed character whose name was now Paul and began to witness for Christ. What an awesome change. (Acts 9: 1-31) Paul began to experience great challenges in the ministry. Regardless of the outcome, he is determined to follow Christ, the anointed One who set him free. From his own words in the book of Romans Paul was inspired to write the following:

> Who shall separate us from the love of Christ? Shall tribulation, or distress, or persecution, or famine, or nakedness, or peril, or sword? As it is written, for my sake we are killed all day long; we are accounted as sheep for the slaughter. In all these things we are more than conquerors through him that loved us. For I am persuaded, that neither death, nor life, nor angels, nor principalities, nor powers, nor things present, nor things to come, nor height, nor depth, nor any other creature, shall be able to separate us from the love of God, which is in Christ Jesus our Lord.

—Romans 8: 35-39

We can take these words literally and apply to our lives. In other words, regardless of the trials and persecution, whatever the accuser of the brethren throws at us we can stand firm and declare that we are redeemed by the blood of Jesus. "No weapon that is formed against you shall prosper; and every tongue that shall rise against you in judgment you shall condemn. This is the heritage of the servants of the Lord . . ." (Isaiah 54:17).

Heavy ministry began for Paul in the midst of some very threatening situations. Here is one example of how Paul handled one dangerous mission that awaited him in Jerusalem. He had a specific purpose when he felt led by the Holy Spirit to go unto Jerusalem, not knowing the things that should befall him there. The disciples had said to Paul through the Spirit that he should not go up to Jerusalem. (Acts 21:4) Nonetheless, through the control of the Holy Spirit, Paul felt compelled to go to Jerusalem. He knew that affliction and suffering awaited him, yet he committed his way to God, not knowing whether it would mean life or death. The Holy Spirit was not forbidding Paul to go to Jerusalem for it was God's will that he go. God, however, was giving Paul a warning that much suffering awaited him if he did go. Nevertheless, Paul counted the cost and was willing even to die for the sake of the Gospel. He relied on the personal guidance of the Holy Spirit and God's Word to him for such an important decision, an example of one sold out to God after his conversion. This is the life of the Christian with a purpose, don't expect milk and honey on the way to kingdom business.

The missionary churches that succeeded are those that did not try to tear down or replace the social fabric of the people they encounter. The Great Commission is to be the primary task of those working in the kingdom, but the Holy Spirit must first empower you. There are a number of unreached people waiting to be evangelized. Our role is to find solutions to reach them wherever they are.

Jesus still leads us by His Spirit to be unique and creative. The Gospel presents Him as an active, compassionate, and obedient servant who, in all circumstances, ministers to the physical and spiritual needs of others. He is one with authority and power, going from one city to another, doing the work of His Father and converting lost souls. Consequently, the congregation needs to be inspired to become excited about missions. As they become involved, personally, they will bring life to the mission world by helping on a local level, to go out into the community and get a glimpse of what is happening out there. The thing that energizes a church and expands its vision is involvement with world missions. Yet, a congregation is often so preoccupied with what happens within its' four walls that it forgets the exciting things God is doing around the world, even though the local church is God's primary method of world evangelization. These churches will not participate, probably because they feel inadequate and refuse to even learn how they can do this. To encourage greater involvement in world missions, one must always define and prioritize. You must have a clear understanding of what missions are, and where to invest your greatest efforts. The mission of the church does refer to everything the Lord has called us to do. In light of this, it is necessary to witness to our neighbors, preach the Word, feed the poor, and carry out a score of other ministries that are supportive to the community. Missions usually involve crossing cultural barriers in an attempt to share the Gospel with people who have little or no opportunity to hear it.

Although the command from the Lord is to evangelize our neighbors, the work of missions calls the church to reach out to the world, to cross barriers of culture and language, and to develop specialized ministries to win people for Jesus Christ. The churches that are missionaries in Africa, India, Asia and the Caribbean Islands have much to report in terms of church growth, through healing, and teaching the Word of God.

The laws and commands of God impose on us an obligation to love Him completely, and to love our neighbor as ourselves. The apostle Paul gives us an example of what it means to be obligated, and why one must become involved in sharing the Gospel. We have heard that Paul made a drastic change through the Gospel. Therefore, he was obligated to share it. The Lord had commanded him to do so. He was totally committed to share the truth that had so radically changed his life. His was the fact that Jesus visited him personally. As a result, he shared this truth with great zeal.

For this reason, I have to share the change in my life as an abusive wife and mother. You don't need to know only one aspect of my life. I must share with you the full story of how I managed to survive hell. It would have been easy to get a divorce, and get on with my life with no stalking, no continued abuse, no fighting in court even though the process was completed many years ago. I wish I could say that was the case with me. I am sure there are many other women out there who went through similar situations, perhaps not quite as brutal. Nonetheless, mine was an abusive marriage, a frightful divorce and continued senseless fights with a sick spouse. Others have settled with an amiable relationship with their spouses after separation, because there was no psychological imbalance in the marriage and no engagement with the devil.

CHAPTER 11

Anger and unforgiveness

Despite the hell one might have gone through, there is a disease that can hold you bound as a result of the abusive relationship. It is called "anger and unforgiveness." It is imperative to rid yourselves of that heavy weight. My deep concern is that it affects many individuals today. There are those who are incarcerated in their minds because of physical and mental abuse, and don't know how to get out of the anger that comes with the territory. I encourage you to read the Word of God on a daily basis for there you will find healing. Let go of that horrible disease called anger and unforgiveness. It is not easy, but mandatory.

The Word of God is replete with healing, and God is faithful to keep His promises. The key is to believe and trust Him for He is able to take care of you, regardless of what is going on in your life. In the Gospel of John, Jesus says: "Peace I leave with you, my peace I give unto you: not as the world gives . . . Let not your heart be troubled, neither let it be afraid" (John 14:27). It is not going to be easy, but help comes when we meditate on the Word of God. In Jesus, you will find a friend, a lover, a Savior, a provider and a peacemaker. He is an awesome God and He, too, experienced much suffering on His earthly journey.

The Scripture says, ". . . He was wounded for our transgressions, he was bruised for our iniquities: the chastisement of our peace was upon him; and with his stripes we are healed." (Isaiah 53:5). It is for this reason we can be confident that God is faithful, who will not give us more than we can bear. Yes, I know it is not as easy as it sounds. Yet, if you hold on to Jesus deliverance will certainly come. It is because I come to know Him I am able to survive the demonic violence that is coming at me. Even so, the Bible is replete with the cure for all our problems. It is for this reason I take the responsibility to help those who are abused and to offer solution for healing. My role is to reach those who still can't find rest for your minds, and a spiritual awareness that Jesus is near and wants to fellowship with you. If reading the Word is not one of your hobbies, have someone go through the Scripture with you on a regular basis. This is vital. You don't have to be in hiding. Stand firm in the liberty where Christ has made you free. You have a promise from God that He will take care of you, no matter what the situation is. Today, He is taking care of me despite the enemy's bombardment.

There are those who choose to commit suicide, some have turned to alcohol, drugs, and others have become catatonic, refusing to move out of their present situation, because there is no one with whom they could communicate. I know there are many others like me out there, but the difference is, someone encouraged me to go to school and to further my education thereby keeping my mind occupied in something positive and keeping busy in the things that are valuable, academically and spiritually. I committed to do that under great affliction because I was bombarded by the enemy. With the help of God, I survived and graduated with two Bachelors' degrees, two Masters' degrees and a Doctorate degree (Ph.D.). I give God the glory for giving me the strength and the courage to make it thus far.

While my spouse was thinking of the next attack on me, and working on the children's minds, I managed to occupy myself in other things that would nourish my mind and spirit. For example, apart from my regular job, I found time to help someone on the mission field.

Unfaithfulness part of his nature

As his regular habit, my spouse did not hesitate to flirt with my friends and co-workers, even in my presence. I watched and kept cool while all this was going on. That should not be a surprise to me because all those characteristics were in place before marriage, when he had an affair with one of my roommates. Even during the marriage we attended a party together with one of my co-workers and her husband. My spouse struggled hard flirting with her while I looked on. He didn't care who got hurt. My co-worker kept looking at me while they were dancing, even as she tried to ignore him. Feeling a little embarrassed, the next day at work she said,

"George was in a high mood yesterday."

"Yes, I know." I replied.

Always know that one day victory and deliverance will come if you put your trust in the one who has your life in His hand. His name is Jesus Christ. The world is full of disappointments and hurts but if you can only take your eye off those disappointments and place it on Jesus Christ, victory is yours. Meanwhile, I will proceed with my assignments, one of which is writing this book. It seems as though it would not materialize because the fight is ongoing. Nonetheless, God is in charge of this work and He wins every time.

Holy Spirit our helper

Jesus says in the book of Acts: "You shall receive power after the Holy Spirit is come upon you: and you shall be witnesses unto me both in Jerusalem, and in all Judea, and in Samaria, and unto the uttermost part of the earth" (Acts 1:8). He specifically instructed His disciples to wait on the Holy Spirit before beginning the ministry. It is imperative that you are filled before getting out on the field where evil shows up frequently. I didn't know that when I began my ministry.

The power of the Holy Spirit was not designed solely for the first-century church. Rather, all Christians are indwelt by the Spirit and thus have His power available. However, living the Christian life under the anointing must not be thought of as simply allowing the Spirit to take control while the believer does nothing. As believers we live the Christian life though we do it through the Spirit's power. To be on the field we are required to be filled with the Holy Spirit. So there is an indwelling for every believer who receives Jesus as Lord of your life.

In addition, we need the infilling in order to survive on the streets and in the nations. This is the reason Jesus commanded His disciples to tarry in the upper room, and wait for the power—the anointing, the promise of the Holy Spirit, before endeavoring the work of the ministry. His instruction was, tarry in the upper room until you are endued with power.

Therefore, 120 disciples obeyed, prayed until the Holy Spirit manifested Himself and saturated them with a powerful anointing. His presence among them became real, and Jesus became known to them in a powerful way. Real power, (Greek: "dunamis"), emphasizes the authority to drive out evil spirits, and heal the sick as the two essential signs accompanying the proclamation of the kingdom of God. The release of the power of the Holy Spirit in the book of Acts in and through the believers' lives caused them to witness with "boldness" and "great power, with many signs, wonders and miracles, and with great results on the mission field.

According to the Scripture, Jesus Himself did not begin His ministry until he had been "anointed with the Holy Spirit and with power: who went about doing good, and healing all that were oppressed of the devil for God was with him" (Acts 10:38). Jesus is a perfect example of the importance of the anointing before embarking on the journey.

The subject of mission is relevant to today's environment in that nations are overwhelmed with the cares of the world. The sound of wars, rumors of wars, economic problems are real. And people are looking for solutions. More than ever, people are committing suicide for various reasons. Some have lost their loved ones through sickness, acts of terror, or war, and are unable to cope without them.

A few years ago, one young person was reaching out on the internet, saying, "Somebody, help me. I'm going to kill myself." Others have actually committed suicide without giving a clue prior to their actions. And so many things maybe happening in the child's mind, of which the parents are not aware, until it is too late.

Mothers are killing their children by drowning them. People are sick mentally, physically and spiritually. The solution is Jesus. However, since they got rid of Him in the schools where children and young people spend much of their time on a daily basis, the outcome has been disastrous. I see prayer as a priority in the homes. Also, educating the community about the importance of inviting Jesus into their lives and into the homes is part of our mission.

Expert on the study of missions

Here is a word from one of the experts in missions. Author of "Leadership Handbooks of Practical Theology," James Berkley, says, "The purpose of missions is the conversion of the lost, the establishment of the church, the restoration of creation, and the glorifying of God's grace throughout the universe forever."

The Great Commission is a call to do just that, to commit our lives to the work of Christ. The goal is that one must be available to move when the call comes, with the ability to adapt oneself to every situation on the mission field, without being offensive to the people with whom one comes in contact. To reiterate, we will come in contact with the poor, the rich, the healthy, the sick, and people who are different in many aspects. The culture might be entirely different, not what we had expected. They all need to be in touch with God and we have the message.

On the mission, I found that there was a great need for love, which seems to be lacking in Christianity. People feel a sense of failure in Christianity and, as a result, are attracted to cults that demonstrate love. They introduce a false god that promises them a sense of hope. You therefore, have to reach them with the truth, which is, to know Jesus Christ.

The churches that work for missions and send out missionaries are themselves truly concerned with one of the most important concerns of God. I am glad to be a part of that missionary endeavor, instead of sitting around and allowing the enemy to think he has power over God's servants. For this reason I believe studying the Word ought to take priority in our lives. For the Word of God penetrates our inner being, it discerns and defines even the dividing line between spirit and soul.

In the New Testament spirit refers to the spiritual dimension of our being, our life in relation to God. Soul or psyche refers to our inner life irrespective of our spiritual experience and our life in relation to us. In other words, our emotions, thoughts and desires and choices are all referring to the soul.

God's Word awakens and strengthens His life in our spirit. It exposes our soulfulness, and sometimes comes in conflict with the life of God within us. By willingly submitting to God's piercing Word, our hearts may be softened and changed so that we may truly enter into God's rest. The alternative is to harden our hearts against God's Word, be condemned by it and perish in unbelief, as did the generation of the Israelites in the wilderness. It reminds us of the seriousness of our choices when responding to God's Word.

During His temptation in the wilderness, Jesus rebuted with the Word, "It is written, man shall not live by bread alone, but by every Word of God" (Luke 4:4). For this reason, healing and deliverance can take place on the mission field as you apply the Word of God in everything you do. The enemy will come against you as he showed himself in Jesus' ministry. However, Jesus left us a great testimony, "It is written . . ." (Luke 4:4). Applying the Scripture to our lives is of paramount importance. It is powerful.

Because of disobedience, we were doomed for destruction, but God sent His Son as a substitute, so that we may have eternal life. We are redeemed by the blood of Jesus. No matter what the adversary tries, the Word says, "For God so loved the world that He gave His only begotten Son, that whosoever believes in Him should not perish but have everlasting life, For God sent not his Son into the world to condemn the world, but that the world through Him might be saved" (John 3:16-17). It is God's unconditional love. However, we have all turned from Him by going our own way, a direction that leads to destruction. Yet He is merciful and compassionate. His arms are outstretched calling us back on tract.

Eager to serve God, the apostle Paul makes a declaration, "But this one thing I do, forgetting those things which are behind, and reaching forth unto those things which are before, I press toward the mark for the prize of the high calling of God in Christ Jesus" (Philippians 3:13-14). A good example for us to follow, not looking back at where we have been, and all the things that transpired in our lives, but looking forward to better things and great reward. Let us press on.

The apostle sees himself as a runner in a race, exerting all his strength and pressing on with intense concentration in order not to fall short of the goal Jesus Christ has set for his life, that perfect oneness with Christ, the Anointed One, who met him on the road to Damascus on his way to persecute the saints of God. Paul changed immediately, from persecutor of the Church to a dynamic servant of the Lord Jesus. After that encounter with Christ, and having a glimpse of the glory of God when "he was caught up into paradise and heard unspeakable words, which was not lawful for a man to utter" (2 Corinthians 12:4), having found himself in 'The Glory,' he resolved that his life, by the grace of God, will be centered on a new life and his determination to press on, and someday gets to see Jesus face to face.

This is a great revelation for all of us if we want to live the abundant life in Christ. Throughout our lives all kinds of distractions and temptations, such as worries, various problems and evil desires threaten to choke off our commitment to the Lord Jesus. Therefore, we need to forget things which are behind, and press forward, leaving the corrupt world and our old life of sin, and reaching forth towards our great salvation in Christ Jesus. His incomprehensible and unconditional love is ours for the taking. God is awesome and invites you to come, without money and without price. It's unconditional in the sense that no condition is attached to his calling you.

There is no price tag. The invitation is free. God calls everybody regardless of who you are and how society sees you. Here is a perfect example. The relationship of the Jews and Samaritans was one of hostility. The Samaritans built their temple on Mount Gerizim, and the Jews' position was that the Samaritans were excluded from eternal life. But Jesus defied the enemy's plan and went to Samaria to bring salvation, knowing they were all God's children. His visit to Samaria to minister to the Samaritan woman at the well was against protocol in the eyes of the Jews. Nonetheless, Jesus is no respect of person. There is no partiality in His ministry, and we are to emulate that example in our lives and on the mission field.

Prophets of old not immune to discouragement

Those of us who have travelled, and those who have ministered even in our backyard, have at some point felt discouraged over lost souls who showed no sign of repenting. Even the prophet Jeremiah was so discouraged that he wept for God's people. Because of his radical message of God's judgment through the coming Babylonian invasion, he led a life of conflict. His own hometown, even the prophets and priests of Jerusalem, threatened his life. He was put in prison, forced to flee from the king, publicly humiliated by the false prophet Hananiah, and thrown into prison. A heartbroken prophet with a heart-breaking message, he says, "My heart within me is broken because of the prophets. All my bones shake. I am like a drunken man, and like a man whom wine hath overcome, because of the Lord, and because of the words of his holiness." "For both prophet and priest are profane, in my house I have found their wickedness, says the Lord" (Jeremiah 23:9, 11).

The prophet's broken heart caused him to write a message that faithfully declared surrendering to God's will is the only way to escape calamity. Jeremiah denounces the sins of the false prophets who had opposed his message of doom, and proclaimed only peace and prosperity. He complained to God, "Ah Lord God! Look, the prophets are telling them, 'you will not see the sword, nor will you have famine,' but I will give you lasting peace in this place." Then the Lord said unto me, "The prophets are prophesying falsehood in my name: I have neither sent them nor commanded them, nor spoken to them. They are prophesying to you a false vision, divination, futility and the deception of their minds" (Jeremiah 14: 13-14 NASB).

And so, God's people must be aware that not all prophets are sent by God. They prophesy lies, and falsely claim to have received visions from the Lord. But there is always a remnant that will remain faithful to God and do His will. Jeremiah faithfully proclaims the divine condemnation of rebellious Judah for 40 years. His reward for this was great opposition, beatings, isolations and imprisonment. His message to the nation of Judah, reads, "Thus says the Lord of hosts, the God of Israel, amend your ways and your deeds, and I will let you dwell in this place" (Jeremiah 7:3 NASB). His sympathy and sensitivity caused him to grieve over the rebelliousness and imminent doom of his nation. He writes, "Oh that my head were waters, and mine eyes a fountain of tears, that I might weep day and night for the slain of the daughter of my people! " (Jeremiah 9:1).

He often desires to be free from the prophetic office because of the hardness of his message and his reception. The Scripture describes him as the weeping prophet, lonely, rejected, and persecuted. However, he perseveres to Judah's horrible end. As he laments over Judah he says, "The harvest is past, the summer is ended and we are not saved" (Jeremiah 8:28). He says, "When I would comfort myself against sorrow, my heart is faint in me, because of the idol worshippers, constantly provoking God to anger with their graven images, and with strange vanities" (Jeremiah 8:18).

Today, we must take the prophet Jeremiah's message seriously. It was a grieving situation for him then, as it is for us today. Yet, I would like to encourage those with the call of God on their lives to move with freedom to serve the true and living God with boldness. When God has a plan for you, no one could stop you. You will have opposition but God will see you through despite the enemy's assaults. I am a living example.

Many years ago, The Lord whispered to me these words, "Being confident of this very thing, that he, who has begun a good work in you, will perform it until the day of Jesus Christ." (Philippians 1:6). These words came at a time when I had been struggling with issues concerning ministry. The Lord showed mercy by encouraging me with this word from the Scripture.

So, regardless of what you are going through, God knows all about it. He will come to your aid. His ways are not our ways. His thoughts are not our thoughts. Seek His face, He will always send you to the Scriptures where you will find a ready-made word to encourage you. Just rest in Him, He has the right prescription for every condition. He can cure your ills, fix your past and prepare you for the mission. He says, Go and I will be with you. There is no need to get locked up in our minds and spirit, and become terrified by the witches who get their authority from Satan. You have the authority from Jesus Christ. Keep your head up and your hands lifted up and God will give you a strategy to come against Satan and his hosts.

There are numerous examples in the Scriptures for everything you are going through. Yes, there is a cure for everything. It is in Jesus Christ. To reiterate, the Scripture reads, "Trust in the Lord with all your heart, and do not lean on your own understanding. In all your ways acknowledge him, and he will make your paths straight" (Proverbs 3: 5-6 NASB). The word trust is mentioned many times in the Scriptures. Still, discouragement can deter you from trusting. But God's Word is true, and we ought to believe it regardless of what the enemy sends our way.

CHAPTER 12

Obstacles part of the territory

Jesus is a perfect example of a reviled and falsely persecuted Christian. The Bible tells us that Christ healed a man who was born blind, and the religious folks of the day, such as the Pharisees and Sadducees took offense because He did the work on a rest day saying, "This man is not from God, because He does not keep the Sabbath" (John 9:16). The reality here is that on the mission, persecution will come. The Scripture says, "For the weapons of our warfare are not carnal, but mighty through God, to pull down strong-holds." (2 Corinthians 10:4). Hence the Holy Spirit is a mighty weapon against the enemy. He is willing to fill us with His anointing before the task. We have to have an upper room experience to be able to survive the trials and persecution we encounter on the field. I was not fully prepared when I started out on the mission, but in a group session I was able to function under the authority of the leader.

These forces that are coming against us are spirits; that is why the Word lets us know, "We wrestle not against flesh and blood, but against principalities, against powers, against the rulers of the darkness of this world, against spiritual wickedness in high places" (Ephesians 6:12). However, there is always a means of retaliation in the Word. Jesus says, "Behold, I give you power to tread on serpents and scorpions, and over all the power of the enemy; and nothing shall by any means hurt you" (Luke 10:19). This power is in the name of Jesus. He has given us the authority to use His name. Let us use that name liberally. Satan respects and is afraid of that name. It is war we are fighting in the atmosphere; we have to deal with these territorial spirits if we are to move forward in God. We must search the Scriptures for therein lies the answer.

So, having to live with an individual who cherishes these demons and refuses to denounce them is unacceptable. This is just to give you an idea of what it means to live in a home where one's spouse deals in heavy witchcraft to control his family.

Christians face spiritual conflict with Satan and a host of evil spirits. These powers of darkness are the spiritual forces of evil that energize the ungodly, oppose the will of God, and frequently attack the believers today. They constitute a great multitude and are organized into an empire of evil with rank and order.

Nevertheless, this is not to frighten you. It is to make you aware of what it is like to live a life without Jesus Christ.

What the world needs is a touch from God, a revival that would affect the people around us, not a utopia, but a place with a genuine need for more of God. That is why the apostle Paul felt this yearning and wrote, "Oh that I may know him, and the power of his resurrection, and the fellowship of his sufferings, being made conformable unto his death" (Philippians 3:10).

It is the desire to get close to Jesus, to surrender totally all that's valuable to us, and love Jesus with a sincere heart, not our emotion but genuine compassion for the one who gave His life, shed His precious blood on Calvary's cross for you and me. His name is Jesus. More specifically, the apostle Peter received the revelation when Jesus asked the disciples:

> "Who do men say that I the Son of man am?"
>
> They answered, "Some say that you are John the Baptist, some Elijah, and others Jeremiah or one of the prophets."
>
> Jesus said unto them, "But whom say ye (you all) that I am?"
>
> Simon Peter answered and said, "Thou art the Christ, the Son of the living God."
>
> —Matthew 16: 13-16

The Scripture lets us know in the book of Philippians 3:6-8, Paul was ready to give up everything for a life of genuine fellowship with Jesus Christ—to be more like Him. He calls those things which were valuable and very special in his life, rubbish, that he may win Christ. That's why he could say in v. 10, "That I may know him, and the power of his resurrection . . . ." Herein is a perfect example of living a virtuous life for the cause of Christ.

We, too, must realize the depth in which we are to communicate with God. Jesus says, "I am in my Father, and you in me, and I in you" (John 14:20).

What an honor and a privilege and a tremendous blessing. If only you can get a picture of whom you are and whose you are in God's sight. This Scripture makes it clear that we are one in Him. We are to embrace that oneness and come to the realization that we are special in God's sight. We are His creation, and are valuable, more than we realize. We live in a time when those with great spiritual resources are falling exhausted, and many believers are discouraged, spiritually and physically. You can run out of spiritual resources and all your formula for building a successful Christian life. Also, building a successful ministry can fail you, so you can become spiritually and mentally drained. Sometimes the frustration of not being able to make contact with spiritual energy through fellowship and prayer can be seen in our attitudes toward people. Meanwhile, we are trying to convince ourselves that our feelings are an attack from the devil or of being let down by authority figures. Ministry has not turned out as expected, leaving us with a feeling of isolation and loneliness. For example, the feeling is such that you dare not share with anyone the doubts and despair you are experiencing.

Sometimes one blames God as well as fellow believers for this emptiness and therefore, the Word does not become a priority in our lives. One becomes preoccupied with self-pity. Yet, the Scripture reads, "Be anxious for nothing, but in everything, by prayer and supplication with thanksgiving let your request be made known unto God" (Philippians 4:6). In other words, you are not to worry about anything or live on murmuring street. Move away from complaining and complainers, so that your attitude becomes positive, generous, lovable and pure. Give it over to Jesus, the Author and Finisher of our faith.

Occasionally, we try to take on too much on ourselves and seem to forget that our helper is in our midst. Don't ever forget the Holy Spirit. He is our counselor, teacher, helper and comforter. In the name of Jesus, you simply need to cry out to Him, "Lord, help me!"

There were times when I had to make this Scripture come alive in my situation. It is important to encourage yourself with the Word of God.

The Apostle Paul's prayer is a prayer that sums up the highest desires of any believer. He writes, "That Christ may dwell in your hearts through faith; and that you being rooted and grounded in love, may be able to comprehend with all saints what is the breath, and length, and depth, and height; and to know the love of Christ, which surpasses knowledge, that you may be filled with all the fullness of God" (Ephesians 3:17-19). In verse 20 he goes on to praise God who exceeds those highest desires, and says, "Now to Him who is able to do exceeding abundantly beyond all that we ask or think, according to the power that works within us." Therefore, even in the midst of your dilemma, you must praise God. He is the one who is able to supply every need even beyond your expectations. Trust and do what He asks. For example:

The Word commands us to "Go . . . ." The command does not depend on feelings, and on our economic status, because God promises to supply all our needs according to His riches in glory. He has asked us to be courageous, as He will be with us to the end of the earth. In addition, doing missionary work on an individual basis, and even traveling to the nations with church groups, can leave you financially depleted and this is where I am today, yet with no regrets. I enjoyed every minute of it.

What could be more rewarding after you have gone through hell at home, to take a new adventure and make it a prize-winning affair to the honor and glory of God? There is nothing more beneficial than getting out there and helping somebody. You will find that you are not the only one with issues beyond your imagination. And a word from you could help others who might be going through all kinds of situations. Sometimes you might feel your problems are such that no one can help you. But remember, no problem is too much for the Lord Jesus.

In India, it was heartbreaking to see the well-dressed Indian woman moving along the streets, and standing next to her was a young Indian girl shabbily dressed with flies buzzing around her. Ministering to this young girl without an interpreter seemed hopeless. Even the name of Jesus seemed foreign to her. As my roommate and I prayed and ministered to her, we found out that her parents had sent her to the streets with the child in her arms to secure provision for the family. So there is always a need greater than yours and you could be an asset by finding a way to help. You will find it rewarding as opposed to staying home and nursing your problems.

The concept of mission according to the Bible, deals with our attitudes towards other people. Not everyone is willing to see change in the community. The story of the prophet Jonah is a good example. God had called him to preach to a nation he despised, so he reacted with disdain. The Scripture tells us that Jonah was sent to Nineveh to deliver a message from God, but Jonah despised the people of Nineveh and knew that God was faithful to forgive them and set them free. Consequently, Jonah refused to deliver the message, and proceeded to hide from God. He soon found out that he or no one could hide from God. He expressed anger and admitted to God that it was better to die than live. (Jonah 4:3). Scripture tells us that "God will have all men to be saved and to come into the knowledge of the truth" (1 Timothy 2:4). The prophet was out of order to decide who should be saved and who should not. God is a God of mercy and compassion. His love does not come with special favor for one individual. Let God do His perfect work in you. If He sends you to a particular people or community, He obviously has plans for them.

God has compassion for the lost. The prophet Jonah did not take kindly to that. In fact, he was angry at God for delivering the people of Nineveh, a wicked nation. To reiterate, the Scripture tells us, God wants none lost. Specifically, Jesus says in the Gospel of Matthew, "It is not the will of your Father who is in heaven, that one of these little ones should perish" (Matthew 18:14). God's compassion is beyond measure. He is patient and gives us ample time to repent of our wicked deeds. It doesn't matter where we live or where we come from, we are all His children.

From a missionary standpoint, I felt the need to help people at home and abroad, but I have been working very hard in the nursing profession and could not even get in the Word of God after a 12-hour shift. I was exhausted. However, every chance I had I delved in the Scriptures. In it there is much food and so much to learn. While you are reading and concentrating on the Word, God shows up with an encouraging word for you personally. He opens doors for you and shows you favor. Here is an example of His favor:

In 1996, I was doing an assignment for my Master's degree in Theology, and a young man was surprised to know I was doing all this work on a typewriter. His parents were buying him a new computer and with their permission he gave me his computer, which was a very small Mac. I had never used a computer before and that was a blessing. I bought a book entitled, "Mac for Dummies," and taught myself how to use the word program. My desire was to learn to type on word, and I managed that well. I was already a typist and was able to do my school assignments using a typewriter. Consequently, using a computer was an asset. A few years later I bought a computer—window PC—where I was able to maneuver the various programs including the internet. Praise God. The awesomeness of God is beyond human expectation. We just need to trust Him.

God is watching out for your health

Even as you are faithful in God's business, He is watching out for you. On the evening shift, on my way home from work, my meals were chicken wings with fried rice. After indulging for many months, the Lord showed me the oil used in the Chinese kitchen. It was black and looked dirty. As a result, I brought the chicken wing dinners to a halt, in obedience to the Lord's command. Later, when my cholesterol became elevated, I attributed that to the nightly Chinese fried food.

Even here, the Lord is faithful to watch my diet while I am running to and fro doing His business. Occasionally, He prescribes other foods for me, mostly beans. So God is watching out for me, even for my health. Certainly, He is doing that for everyone if we will pay attention to Him. Thank God for His faithfulness. Despite our attitudes towards Him, He finds a place for us in redemption—redemption through personal faith in Jesus Christ as Savior and Lord. God justifies all. The Word lets us know in the book of Romans, "Therefore being justified by faith we have peace with God through our Lord Jesus Christ" (Romans 5:1). To be justified is to be declared righteous. Christ has redeemed us by His precious blood. He has redeemed us back to God, so that we are no more strangers but heirs, heirs with God and joint heirs with Jesus Christ.

Redemption through Christ's forgiveness and the entrance of the Holy Spirit into your life brings personal renewal that affects all spheres of life. A good example is found in Second Corinthians, and it reads:

"Therefore if anyone is in Christ, he is a new creation; old things have passed away, behold all things have become new" (2 Corinthians 5:17). Newness in Christ leads not only to inward change or outward practice of personal loyalty, but also to new expressions of love and justice, growing concern for social injustice, and sensitivity to cultural corruption. Christians are called to a life of spirit-empowered holiness that is not only inward, but also outward, and social in nature. The Scriptures are replete with examples of this.

In his first letter to the Corinthians, the apostle Paul was writing to a church that was in trouble, a church that had enough conflict to keep counselors and ministers busy for years. He did not hesitate to express his anxiety for this church. This church was not what he had envisioned when he started it. Paul expressed concerns about the lack of Christian values and relationships, division in the church, conflict as to who the Corinthian Christians should be following, sexual immorality, lawsuits among believers, conflict in marriage and over divorce, the worshipping of idols, and people's lack of love for each other. The apostle was also concerned about the conflicts between those who believed Christians were at odds about how people came together to participate in the Lord's Supper, and the role of women in worship. Their conflict also related to spiritual gifts, and to the lack of unity among believers. In his second letter, he reminded them that they had been reconciled and are still being reconciled, and that they were to continue to engage in a ministry of reconciliation. It is important to remember that through the blood of Jesus all mankind is reconciled to God. But here Paul was especially concerned about human relationships, and sought to encourage unity among them.

This ministry of reconciliation is necessary in every area of our lives such as the families and the workplace where we spend most of our time. Even in the church, conflict is evident. But God has called us to reconciliation. He demands it as a ministry in itself. I cannot stress enough how important this is, as I watched what it had done to others, even those close to me.

At this point I would like to give a biblical definition of the word "reconciliation" taken from Conflict Management by Lowery and Myers. This is a better explanation than in Strong's concordance. Four Greek words help us understand the New Testament concept of reconciliation.

The first word, **"katallasso,"** means to change from enmity to friendship. This means a change in relationship from one of hostility to one of friendship, as in a husband and wife situation. We read in the Scripture, "And unto the married I command, yet not I but the Lord, let not the wife depart from her husband: but if she depart let her remain unmarried, or be reconciled to her husband."

—1 Corinthians 7:10-11

The second Greek word, **"apokatallasso,"** means to reconcile completely. Going further than katallasso, it suggests that all enmity and impediment to peace is removed. The Scripture reads, "And having made peace through the blood of his cross, by him to reconcile all things unto himself."

—Colossians 1:20

The third Greek word that translates as reconcile is the word **"diallassomai."** It means to bring about an alteration—to change, to reconcile in cases of mutual hostility, yielding to mutual concession. Example from the Scripture, "Leave there your gift before the altar, and go your way, first to be reconciled to your brother; and then come and offer your gift."

—Matthew 5:24

The fourth Greek word, a noun, is **"katallage."** It means a change on the part of one person, induced by an action of another. It is most often used to describe the reconciliation of human beings to God through God's love expressed by Christ. The Scripture clarifies this: ". . . we also joy in God through our Lord Jesus Christ, by whom we have now received the atonement or reconciliation."

—Romans 5:11

Another Greek word found in Strong's concordance is **"hilaskomai."** Scripture explains it: "Wherefore in all things it behooved him to be made like unto his brethren, that he might be a merciful and faithful high priest in things pertaining to God, to make reconciliation for the sins of the people."

—Hebrews 2:17

When Jesus considered conflict in the community of believers, He suggested a three-step process for its resolution, which He explains in Scripture, "If your brother sins against you go and show him his fault just between the two of you. If he listens to you, you have won your brother over. But if he will not listen, take one or two others along, so that every matter may be established by the testimony of two or three witnesses. If he refuses to listen to them, tell it to the church, and if he refuses to listen even to the church, treat him as you would a pagan or a tax collector."

—Matthew 18:15-17

In this, Jesus sets forth the method of restoring or disciplining a professing Christian who sins against another member of the church, in a private manner. To neglect Christ's instruction is to compromise the Gospel and induce ultimate destruction to the church as a holy people of God. The purpose of church discipline is to guard the moral purity and doctrinal integrity of the church, and to attempt to save the soul of the wayward member and restore him to fellowship. Of course, church discipline must be carried out in the spirit of humility, love and self-examination. For God's love constrained us to love unconditionally.

Summary of missionary outreach

Effective and meaningful community outreach requires a healthy attitude toward mission and the community around us. One must be committed to the mission field before embarking on such ministry. The effectiveness depends on whether or not you are people oriented. Many church members say that the mission field is not for them. That is understandable, because not everyone is compassionate toward society due to cultural background, fear, and a host of other reasons. But there are those who are strictly mission oriented. In fact, they will tell you this is where their hearts are. But they lack support and encouragement, mostly because the church they attend may not be mission oriented.

One thing to keep in mind is that you cannot serve people without being concerned about their needs, both spiritual and physical. Jesus was at the embodiment of His ministry on earth. He knew when to minister to physical needs, and when to minister to one's spiritual needs. The mission field is ripe for compassion and understanding. I can bear witness to this on my journey. I am sure that missionaries who are working throughout the world can attest to the fact that people are looking for care, not only for themselves but also for their families and for the community as a whole. This situation is heightened in this economical turmoil throughout the nation.

Those who are reaching their communities with the love of Jesus will find the need for prayer high on their list of priorities. Prayer for jobs, prayer for salvation for themselves and their families, including their children, are high on those lists.

Jesus gives an invitation to all who are walking in darkness. He says, "I am the light of the world, he that follows me shall not walk in darkness but shall have the light of life" (John 8:12). This means, without Jesus in your life there will always be a feeling of unrest in your spirit. Dark moments will cause you to become frustrated, with a lack of peace in your life.

Jesus shed His blood so that we can have abundant life. Finally, He arrived at Calvary, hung on the wooden cross, whose final words were, "It is finished" (John 19:30). Because of the finished work on the cross, Jesus took our burdens and nailed them to that cross. This means no weapon formed against us will prosper. Our authority is in the name of Jesus and in the written Word. Jesus completed the finished work at Calvary. Hallelujah!

CHAPTER 13

Assigned to teach

After completing my Master's Degree in theology, I began to teach in the Bible school in Brooklyn, New York. The challenge was tremendous. The students were eager to learn and we had a great relationship. As an anointed school, we had the freedom to pray before and at the end of each class session. God moved in those prayer sessions every time.

I remember teaching one morning on September 11, 2001 and looking out of the windows we could see some of the buildings in Manhattan. We looked and saw the first plane hit the tower. Suddenly the building began to crumble right before our eyes. It was a horrible experience and was rather difficult trying to finish the teaching that morning even though, at the time, we did not have any information as to the seriousness of what happened, until we were in a position to have all the information and to assess the damage resulted from that terrorism. It was sad to hear of the lives that were lost and the way the employees pooled together to jump from the building, in an attempt to escape that extreme heat that emitted from the plane at the time. I sensed they died before hitting the ground because of fear and the height from which they were traveling. What an experience for the students and me in the classroom that day, as we looked at the buildings in that area of Manhattan and tried to make sense of what was taking place. It was horrible. The damage occurred as a result of this tragedy was unthinkable. I shudder when I think of the children and families at home possibly asking the question, "Mummy, when is daddy coming home? Or, Daddy, when is mummy coming home?"

Those wives or husbands, sisters or brothers, mothers or daughters, or sons, who suffered psychologically resulting from that tragedy, need our continued prayer and intervention even today. Some have been hit so hard, they could still feel the damage done to their lives and their families. Their lives are so crushed, and there is a constant reminder of what transpired that day, when the pain keeps recurring. Despite all that, we cannot give up on God or blame Him for that tragedy. The devil would like us to blame God, but many of us know his scheme. He is a liar.

As we lay a wreath every year and call the names of the lost, we are reminded of our loved ones with the hope that one day we will meet in glory. Meanwhile, we need to commune with God continuously, because sudden death can meet us anywhere.

Prayer, a priority

If you feel there is never a need for prayer because your loved ones were not affected, just think of this tragedy and remind yourself, there is always someone or some condition for which we ought to pray. We can be guaranteed peace even in this situation provided we hold on to Jesus, the one who suffered, shed His blood, and gave His life for us. He says in the Scripture, "Let not your heart be troubled, believe in God believe also in me. In my Father's house are many mansions, if it were not so, I would have told you. I go to prepare a place for you, and if I go and prepare a place for you I will come again, and receive you unto myself that where I am, there you may be also" (John 14:1-3).

This is good consolation. God only knows where I would be without a life of prayer. He has been a source of strength to me. According to the Scripture, "He is strength to the needy in his distress, a refuge from the storm, a shadow from the heat . . ." (Isaiah 25: 4).

Herein is an example that you cannot do anything apart from God. The Lord Jesus in the Gospel proclaimed, "I can of mine own self do nothing: as I hear, I judge: and my judgment is just because I seek not my own will, but the will of the Father who has sent me" (John 5:30). Clearly, then, we cannot fight the battle by ourselves. We will die in the process. We can do absolutely nothing without God.

To reiterate, before Jesus went back to heaven He encouraged His disciples with these words, "Peace I leave with you, my peace I give unto you: not as the world gives . . . . Let not your heart be troubled, neither let it be afraid" (John 14: 27). If we follow what is going on in the world we would never have peace, unless the Word of God takes priority in our lives.

It is worth living a life pleasing to God so that when we enter heaven, we know for certain we are going to hear these words, "Well done, good and faithful servant: You have been faithful over a few things, I will make you ruler over many things: enter into the joy of your Lord" (Matthew 25: 21, 23).

Many individuals are in distress because of the economic situation, and many other reasons known to them alone. But Jesus Christ is the answer to all our problems. As we acknowledge the Lord as our source, and exalt Him, we will experience a sense of peace and fulfillment. He is still the most awesome person in our lives. The Scripture acknowledges Him as the bread of life. These are His words: "I am the bread of life: He who comes to me shall never hunger; and he who believes on Him shall never thirst" (John 6:35). As the bread of life, He fed a multitude with five barley loaves and two fishes; so we certainly can depend on Him to fulfill our needs.

Christ is the sustenance that nourishes spiritual life, and it is not His will that any individual should perish, "but that all should come to repentance." He will have all men to be saved, and to come to the knowledge of the truth (2 Peter 3:9; 1Timothy 2:4). "For there is one God and one mediator between God and men, the man Christ Jesus, who gave himself a ransom for all . . . ." (1Timothy 2:5-6)

We continue to have spiritual life as we remain in fellowship with Christ. The Lord says, "The words that I speak onto you, they are spirit, and they are life" (John 6:63). He also says, "If you abide in me and my words abide in you, you shall ask what you will and it shall be done unto you" (John 15:7). This is the prerequisite; abide in the Lord Jesus by staying in the Word as your daily diet. What a privilege and a blessing to know that there is one pre-requisite for a positive response from the Lord Jesus. Simply stay close to Him by spending time in His Word on a daily basis. In other words, have fellowship with Jesus.

Life-style change

There comes a time in your life when you have to make changes, and my time has come to do just that. After 40 years in New York, the cold weather was really affecting me and I felt the need for a change. I thought of moving to Grenada, but decided to stay here in America where the health care system is more feasible as opposed to the Caribbean Islands. So, I relocated to Florida. Thank God for America.

I didn't know anyone here, but soon became acquainted with faithful people who assisted me in getting settled in my home. I began to assist in a Bible school here in Florida and assigned to teach the Master's degree program. I enjoy teaching. In fact, the Lord has anointed me to teach. However, the enemy continues to get in the way, but the one with the greater power must win. His name is Jesus Christ, the Son of God. He says at His temptation in the wilderness, "It is written, man shall not live by bread alone, but by every word of God" (Luke 4:4). We take Him at His Word, so that we can experience the victory.

When the enemy comes against me one way, I turn to my source, Jesus Christ, the Lord and Master of my life. There is power in that name, and in that precious blood that was shed at Calvary. Here is an appropriate and famous chorus from the song-writer regarding the blood of Jesus. I pray that this will minister to your heart as you sing it to the honor and glory of God. Search for the music and begin to sing to your hearts' desire. It ministers to me.

There is power, power, wonder-working power
In the blood of the Lamb;
There is power, power, wonder-working power,
In the precious blood of the Lamb

—Lewis E. Jones

Prayer continues to be the key to our situation. A prayer that does not speak specifically to our need will not suffice. When facing the adversary who "comes to steal and to kill, and to destroy" (John 10:10a), we have to take authority in the Word of God. Jesus says, "I am come that they might have life, and that they might have it more abundantly" (John 10:10b). God has given us the authority. This authority is in the name of Jesus. Take God at His Word. He asks us to trust Him. Again, the Scripture tells us, "Trust in the Lord with all your heart and lean not onto your own understanding; in all your ways acknowledge him, and he will direct your path" (Proverbs 3:3-5). The Lord has encouraged me with this word a few years ago. He is constantly feeding me with Scriptures and songs. An awesome God He is.

Close relationship to Jesus

Just as the apostle Paul described his relationship to Christ in terms of a profound attachment to and reliance upon the Lord, we too have a responsibility to rely on Him totally for spiritual nourishment, physical strength and faith to move on, despite the persecution. We have to be connected to the right source—the heavenly source, Christ Jesus. Knowing Him will keep us hungry for more of Him. As our Good Shepherd, we can depend on Him to care for His sheep. He is Lord and God, lover of our soul, our protector.

Those who have faith in Christ live their lives in intimate union with their Lord, both in His death and resurrection. This means, all believers have been crucified with Christ. We "died to the law that we might live unto God" (Ephesians 2:19). Because of salvation in Christ, sin no longer has dominion over us. The Scripture says, "Likewise, reckon you also yourselves to be dead indeed unto sin, but alive unto God through Jesus Christ our Lord" (Romans 6:11). So don't let the enemy put a guilt trip on you. If you are a true believer you have died to sin, meaning, that the believer's union with Christ in both His death and life, died to sin in God's sight. You are considered by God to have died with Christ and have been raised up in His resurrection.

Consequently, Christ gave us His power to resist sin. We die to sin daily by putting to death the misdeeds of the body and having the confidence, love and devotion, and the loyalty in the Son of God who loved us and gave His life for us. "For God so loved the world, that he gave his only begotten Son, that whosoever believes in him should not perish, but have everlasting life" (John 3:16). What a love, it is unconditional. In other words, you don't have to work for it.

His love is not for sale. It does not depend on where you received your education, or how smart you are, or how much Scripture you can memorize. It's an uncompromising love of God who looked at his creation as completely lost, stretched forth His hand and pulled us out of that hell-bound pathway and said, 'devil, you cannot have them, they are mine.'

What an awesome God we serve. We can depend on Him to deliver us in your day-to-day encounter with the enemy. Very often, as I mentioned before, the Lord consoles me with a word from the Scripture and with a song. I make a note of the songs and try them at the piano. I find this one most appropriate as the Lord brings it at the right moment when I am at my lowest point of my life. It is called, "Joy unspeakable and full of glory."

"There is joy unspeakable and full of glory,
Full of glory, full of glory;
It is joy unspeakable and full of glory,
Oh the half has never yet been told."

—The Lord Jesus

I am really beginning to understand why the Lord insists that I get back to my music. It seems quite a job trying to do both writing and music. I know the writing is ordained of God and the music is, also. I wish I could discipline myself to give them both the same attention. But as much as I love music, the inconsistency has been tugging at me over the years. I should have been an expert at the piano, but without adequate practice one cannot accomplish that goal.

CHAPTER 14

On the battlefield

A review

When I think of what is really happening in the marriage, to the neighbors, friends and co-workers, life at home is heavenly. We must look good—a perfect couple, an example of a perfect marriage. Little do they know, an example of hell transcends the life of this individual. I dare not tell anybody about the hell I am experiencing at home. I must keep my lips sealed with a ready-made smile on my face while I move through the community. It is as though the adversary is saying, "Serve me, or die!" Yet, there is no one with whom I could confide. In this situation one feels trapped, especially when a spouse expects his wife to put on a smile even with an obvious black eye.

When one is facing the issue of one spouse either selling his own children to the devil, or the wife facing the possibility of such sacrifice herself, her only hope is in Jesus Christ. I write this book in an attempt to prepare you for what might be possible in your marriage and how you can handle it with the strength of the Lord Jesus. He promises to be at your side, and will not leave you comfortless, despite the pressure. Sharing your concerns with Him, you will not have to turn to alcohol, drugs or suicide. Jesus has accomplished what He had set out to do despite the many obstacles He encountered during His ministry. Scripture says, "When He had disarmed the rulers and authorities, He made a public display of them, having triumphed over them through Him" (Colossians 2:15 NASB). He nailed them to the cross. We, too, must not let the devil stop our progress.

It is with a humble spirit I write this book as God is encouraging me to do so. It is an overwhelming decision and a hard task. However, telling this truth is of the utmost importance, especially since so many spouses are going through this kind of punishment and don't know how, or don't want to seek help for fear of drastic punishment by their spouses. So they suffer and end up with suicidal tendencies. Many continue the relationship because of the children, especially when young children are involved in the battle.

If you look around, you will find yourself asking the question, "Where do I go from here?" The evil is like a vehement fire, ready to consume your young ones. Parents fail to detect this until the children act it out in the schools, even on the bus as they travel to school. It is for this reason prayer is so vital at home where the children can experience a praying family and learn to pray themselves when the occasion arises.

For this reason, growing up with the stigma from the abusive surroundings in the home, results in psychological problems. Even adults are not exempt from the evil that follows as a result of childhood abuse. The treatment that many spouses have to endure is astounding and horrifying. Yet, to all appearances everything is perfect.

To reiterate, it is up to us to develop a relationship with the Lord Jesus, because we will need His help to overcome the tragedies of life. If I did not have a personal relationship with Him I would not be able to stand, and any decision I make maybe unfruitful.

A constant battle

I worked feverishly to help maintain the home. After establishing a home and citizenship, the children were doing well in school despite what was happening at home. In 1966, two years after we came to America, we bought a car. This was part of my transportation to and from work. I drove to the shopping center downtown Brooklyn, called to let my spouse know where I was and that I had the car with me, the sound at the other end of the telephone died, as though a sudden storm had come and passed immediately. I decided to break the silence. "Are you there?" I asked. There was a complete change in the conversation because I was out of order to take the car. In fact, I was not capable of doing anything substantial by myself. That included handling the new car. So my using the car delivered an electric shock to my spouse's brain causing him to go into silent mode for a moment. However, I was glad to be home safely, with no damage to the car. Instead, I developed a sense of responsibility to know that I could handle myself without fear.

Despite all this, it is important to be in touch with God. Confess our pride and failures to God and invite the Lord Jesus into our hearts, He guarantees a peace that passes all understanding; not the peace that the world gives, that's transient and only available when things go well. I am talking about the peace that comes from God during our darkest hour.

The Lord has been my peace in the midst of my circumstances, and He ministers to me frequently in songs and in the Word. Today, He wakes me up and ministers to me in the wee hours of the morning. Sometimes He gives me a Scripture from the Old Testament, and at other times He gives me a Scripture from the New Testament. He does this very often, and lets me know that "He is the light of the world." He shines in my life on a daily basis. John, the beloved apostle said in the Gospel that

Jesus was that true light. If ever we needed that light, it is now. Jesus comes in His fullness, flooding me with sweetness and warmth like I have never known. I see Him as loving, caring, living, forgiving and imparting to my soul His very being—new life, new strength, new hope. He is all that we have and all that we need. He is our only hope. His name is Jesus, the Christ, the Son of God.

Your parent's advice is valuable

Many years ago, my father had written to me with a fatherly concern about getting married to someone without doing a background check. My answer infuriated him. "I don't need you to investigate." I replied. I had not since spoken to Daddy until I visited him in the hospital following a stroke. He was not responsive but indicated that he was able to hear me, for he looked around the room, his eyes roaming for a glimpse of me, but couldn't speak.

"Daddy, I'm here." I said. Obviously, he could hear every word I was saying. He died nonetheless without our communicating to each other. At the time I had no knowledge of forgiveness and reconciliation and what it can do to the soul, until I came to know Jesus as Lord of my life. I needed to repent and straighten things out with Daddy. At the time of his death I was already divorced. Before that I was not able to make a trip to Grenada to see him, since he questioned me about the man I married. Even at the funeral it didn't seem to matter, but as I matured in the knowledge of God and realized the importance of making things right, I had to settle any dispute, so that I could be free in mind and spirit. In this case I had to settle it with God as Daddy was no longer here on earth.

The fight is on even in the 1990's

My eldest daughter was the only one remained faithful to me because of what she witnessed during the marriage. I always felt she was the one who saved my life on many occasions during physical abuse. Suddenly, there was a change in her attitude. I wrote a letter begging and asking her the reason for her change of attitude towards me. I wrote, telephoned many times, with no response. I suddenly came to the conclusion that her father had taken care of that after our last appearance in court. The judge had put him in his rightful place when he subpoenaed me to appear in court, accusing me of owing him money.

This final trip to court 20 years after the divorce temporarily put a stop to the madness. But of course he has to continue his efforts to bind the children to the devil. He didn't get his way in court so the girls must never speak to me or see me ever. He did a job on their minds. Despite the letter to my daughter and her refusal to talk with me, she complained to a family member that I refused to get in touch with her. Can you see what's happening here? Obviously she is under the control of the evil one.

Years later and after much prayer, I managed to get her to the phone, and we had a good conversation. All ended well, but the next two weeks there was no response. However, I contacted her through the mail to let her know what I thought the enemy was doing in our lives. Their father will not stop until he destroys everyone who gets in the way of their knowing the truth. Already he has destroyed many individuals to satisfy his habit with the devil.

Jesus spoke much about Satan and his demons and the spiritual warfare in which we, as His servants, will face. Professing Christians who try to deal with the ravages of satanic rituals without the power of Jesus Christ, are clearly demonstrating the fact that they are neglecting the Word of the Lord. They are afraid that they will lose credibility in the eyes of the world and be considered crazy because of a stand for Jesus.

After His resurrection, Jesus said to His disciples, "Go into the entire world, and preach the gospel to all generation. He who has believed and has been baptized shall be saved; but he who has disbelieved shall be condemned, and these signs will accompany those who have believed: In my name they shall cast out demons; they will speak with new tongues. They will pick up serpents, and if they drink any deadly poison, it shall not hurt them; they shall lay hands on the sick, and they will recover" (Mark 16: 15-18 NASB). It is clear then that these evil exist and we are to take authority over them in the name of Jesus. However, to do so we must have proper understanding and instruction through the Word of God. It is spending time with Jesus, having fellowship with Him on a daily basis.

Ritualistic child abuse

Having studied this kind of abuse, it is interesting to note that ritualistic child abuse is not a new phenomenon. The children experience satanic ritual and is usually repeated more than once, depending on the circumstances. The purpose of this type of abuse is always to place demons within the child. The demons then exercise a profound influence on the child's growth and development, frequently almost totally controlling them. The problem of ritualistic child abuse is not a subject that is frequently discussed but it happens regularly throughout the nations where there is heavy witchcraft.

My four adult daughters were invited to spend Christmas on the Island of Grenada with their father and his wife. At this time they are adults, some with their own children. I am not in authority to say what transpired on the Island, but looking at the situation where there is no release, I don't want to even think of the possibilities of what might have transpired during that vacation.

However, research shows that children and even adults, subjected to such rituals are always diagnosed by various psychotherapists, psychologists and or psychiatrists as multiple personalities or schizophrenic. In fact, the multiple personalities are demons. Until this is recognized and dealt with through the power of Jesus Christ, little help is possible for the victims. Left untreated, the child grows up to adulthood and enters the marriage with uncontrollable behavior. Demons can only be dealt with in the power and authority of Jesus Christ. Psychiatry is completely helpless to do anything with demons.

Jesus sees the world and society in which we live as an "adulterous and sinful generation." All those who seek to be popular in or accepted by their present evil generation rather than follow Christ and His righteous standards will be rejected by Christ at His return. Now it is up to us to walk in a relationship with the Lord Jesus whereby we, too, can triumph over these powers and authorities in the precious name, and wonderful power of Jesus Christ.

Again, If we do not have a personal relationship with the Lord, we will not be able to stand, and any decision me make will most likely be unfruitful. For example, God is encouraging me to write this book, and when obstacles get in the way of my progress, the Lord gives me a word from the Bible to encourage me and to let me know that He is aware of what I am dealing with, and that my strength comes from Him. I read and meditate on the Scriptures He gives me and find comfort in them.

My hope is that this book will enlighten you, especially those who are experiencing trials in your relationships. Jesus accomplished victory for you on the cross when He suffered and died over 2000 years ago. Now it is up to you to walk in a relationship with the Lord whereby you, too, can triumph over these powers in the precious name and in the power of Jesus Christ.

CHAPTER 15

A child of divorced parents

Divorce after an abusive marriage is extremely difficult for the entire family. It hurts all members of the family, and sometimes the wounds of divorce are deep, and take years to heal. There are various kinds of abusive marriages. One can be abused emotionally in the marriage, but difficult to explain. Physically, abusive marriages sometimes result in death.

To understand the real meaning of abuse one has to explain it from one's own experience. Accordingly, arguing and neglecting is not considered abuse. In my estimation this is insignificant in terms of what I have been going through. I believe one can tolerate this kind of behavior as long as there is no physical damage. Many of you might disagree with me, but I am just being personal. Being severely hurt physically and or mentally is what I am dealing with at this time. Calling names are known as verbal abuse. Again, I believe I can deal with that. For example, abuse may start when the couple tries to sort out an argument in a harsh manner and because of the tone of one individual, a flaring up could ensue causing a huge blast of what should have been a simple dialogue between the two. This can lead to harsh words or even physical abuse. Although a simple argument between parents can affect the emotional health and well-being of the child, divorce can be very damaging as the child feels scared and does not want to part from the parents. Without counseling this can lead to unpleasant consequences. For example, one might refuse to communicate and become depressed, leading to other diseases. In fact, the action of the parents after the divorce often disturbs children even more than the adults. I am speaking from experience. During an argument, the action of the parents depends on the level of maturity of the individuals.

Therefore, you need to be extremely careful about how you behave with your child while surviving divorce. I believe the most difficult situation is where there is evil, such as one parent holding the children hostage through witchcraft, as a means of having some control. This is immature, and depicts insecurity on the part of that parent.

Also, it's very hard for the children since their basic security is threatened by what is happening around them. The children need and seek out both parents. One of my daughters specifically said in answer to such a question by her father, "I want both of you." She replied. Sometimes it's hard to stay cool and maintain your sanity when one partner will not let you rest by becoming attached to witchcraft. Again, it shows weakness and insecurity on behalf of that spouse.

No man in his right mind will turn to this kind of evil to control his children and try to ruin their mother. It's a real sickness, a mental problem. Children don't want to hear anything bad about a parent since they are equally loyal to both. They will feel betrayed if you prohibit them from meeting a parent and will move away from you emotionally. In my case, they were not given a chance to display such emotions. They were bound by the demons that were placed in them.

Trying to change any legal arrangements will get the child confused. In my case their father refused to accept the legal arrangement by the court and threatened to kill them all if I were to remove them from the home. I didn't care about the $45.00 a week for child support; improving my life by getting out of that hell took priority over the money. The court had already made the decision that I have custody of the children. Nonetheless, the fight has just begun as their father says, "No."

Something went wrong in my life and I take it as a lesson and learn from it. If you are finding it difficult to cope with your preexisting condition, it is essential that you seek help as this is available for you in America. As a nurse, I speak with authority as I witness this in the nursing profession. A social worker is always available, willing and ready to listen to your needs with compassion, and making sure you are referred to the appropriate authority for assistance. This happens as a result of your being in the hospital for a medical problem, but the nurse or physician observes an entirely different situation that calls for concern.

What goes on in the home where one is not permitted to talk about, you are left at the mercy of the abuser. In some cases the victim's concern for her mental and physical well-being is very real and as such, victims learn to exercise extreme caution, so as not to set off their abusive partner. Hence, these persons learn to walk circumspectly, very mindful of their own behavior as well as their partner's mood so as to avoid raising issues that may be risky. This is how I managed to escape alive, with a sense of worth.

Leaving requires a plan

Does it make sense to plan before you leave? Many articles on abusive marriage suggest "plan before you leave." The objective in a departure from an abusive situation is your safety and that of your children. So leaving requires a plan. The first step in planning is finding support. I believe support is always available, but to reiterate, I looked for support from the police and can assure you, that was not a worthwhile choice in New York. Family court is the place where everybody goes in cases like these, but I was living with an abuser and it required much courage to travel to family court and spend probably one whole day before being able to see and speak to someone in that organization. And once it is established that I was being abused, they would most likely get my spouse out of the house. I could see these small children grieving over their father's absence from the home. My settlement was based on achieving peace at any cost. But is there going to be peace at the end of this trial? Read on.

To achieve that I consulted an attorney who worked diligently to ensure an amiable outcome. With a spouse that objects to the divorce, objects to counseling, yet continues the abuse senselessly, just does not make room for conciliatory outcome. It is amazing how God has blessed me with a mind to stand up to these kinds of treatment. I thank God for His goodness and His mercy towards me, as I was able to survive and come out of this relationship alive and sane.

The Scripture says, "And be not conformed to this world, but be transformed by the renewing of your mind, that you may prove what is that good and acceptable, and perfect, will of God" (Romans 12:2). Your mind is the battleground. The enemy finds it easy to play with your mind, and looks for the opportunity to throw fiery darts in that direction. So, it is vital to stay in the Word of God, and meditate on it constantly.

Of course, my continuing in this freedom is a threat to the enemy. Even though my spouse promised I "will never be happy with another man," I used the time and energy to better myself and enter a degree program, both academically and theologically. I am truly blessed even though my spouse is disturbed even more to find that I am still alive, in Jesus.

After a divorce you would think peace awaits you as you move to new direction. However, the abuser may find other strategy to continue his abusive practice. In my case my spouse had no intention of taking his hands off the filth with which he has indulged for many years, probably all his life for that matter. For this reason, I can definitely attest to the fact that abuse after divorce is not strange, especially when you are dealing with what seems to be a schizophrenic character. This is exactly what is happening even today after the many years of what I thought was, a road to freedom from abuse.

Typically, according to research, when exiting a relationship, the person looking for power and control over the other will escalate his tactics out of fear of losing his power and authority. The fact that I have developed some stamina and realized I do not have to tolerate this kind of treatment any more, has caused my spouse to escalate his tactics. Money was his to explore and control while we were together, even when the abuse was in effect. That was all right with me.

It's amazing to think that one's spouse could take the liberty of abusing his wife and expects her to just humbly succumb to that kind of behavior almost on a daily basis, without complaining or doing anything about it. I say this because he was very daring to think and even to express, that I would not be able to handle separation because he has been handling the moneys throughout the marriage.

The idea is that I would be lost without him. On the contrary, he now comes to the realization that I can take care of myself in the name of Jesus. I used those paychecks to buy a home since he insisted on having our present home. He was stunned to know I could buy a home and handle the transaction, all to the honor and glory of God. This was where he came and proposed to me for the second time, on my door steps. Whether or not he expected to move into my new home, or come back to the home which is now his, I would have been out of my mind to get back in that prison cell. Yes, I was living in a hellish prison. How incredible even to imagine this could go on until I get to heaven and expect a gold medal from the Lord for being able to tolerate massive abuse.

Even so, I had no intention of entering God's domain with a disfigured body. No-no-no! There is a dream deep down in my belly, and God is about to fulfill that dream. I didn't know about it at the time because I was not in the place to hear from God. Nonetheless, as soon as I began to read the Bible and realize Jesus is my Lord, I began to experience a sense of belonging and peace. I developed an attitude of listening to Him. As a result, I began to hear from the Lord. Oh, how unsearchable are His ways. They are past finding out. He gives me a song and a Word from the Bible just to let me know He is here looking after me. In essence, God is saying to me, be of good courage. I see what you are going through. The Bible says, "Surely goodness and mercy shall follow me all the days of my life: and I will dwell in the house of the LORD forever" (Psalm 23:6). This is the consolation we have in the Word of God.

Violence is not a new phenomenon

Violence has always been a feature of the relationship, and the severity or intensity continues even today, with the children under the control of the devil.

I entered the relationship with my eyes wide open, with no one to blame. Nonetheless, God is always working behind the scene, pulling things together and making everything materialize according to His plan and purpose. One pastor says it just right. If God gives you a vision, it's up to Him to bring it to fruition, as long as the function would include kingdom business. Engaging in kingdom business is the key to having victory in your life. Instead of worrying about the attacks that are coming against you, get busy in having fellowship with the Lord. He will see you through this entire ordeal.

God is good. What a wonderful Savior He is. We can rest in Him. The Scripture says, "Rest in the Lord, and wait patiently for him: fret not yourself because of him who prospers in his way, because of the man who brings wicked devices to pass" (Psalm 37:7). This means, regardless of what you are going through, don't give up. Hold on like Jacob who wrestled with the angel of the Lord, saying "I will not let you go except you bless me" (Genesis 32: 26). Be patient. Your day of victory will come. I am prophesying to you today. As you read this book I encourage you, hold on to God's promises and pursue your dream. Stay in the Word, meditate on it day and night and God will give you a strategy. When He does, write it down. Get on your computer and begin to write. As you move, the information will begin to flow naturally. Don't fix it as you go along. Don't concern yourself with the way it sounds. You can edit and make corrections later. In fact, I am sharing my testimony. I set this writing aside because the enemy tried its utmost to block me. Nevertheless, I kept musing over Ephesians Chapter Six and got hold of that Scripture which says:

> Finally, my brethren, be strong in the Lord, and in the power of his might. Put on the whole armor of God that you may be able to stand against the wiles of the devil. For we wrestle not against flesh and blood, but against principalities, against powers, against the rulers of the darkness of this world, against spiritual wickedness in high places. Where-fore, take unto you the whole armor of God that you may be able to withstand in the evil day, and having done all, to stand. Stand therefore, having your loins girt about with truth, and having on the breastplate of righteousness, and your feet shod with the preparation of the gospel of peace; Above all, taking the shield of faith, wherewith you shall be able to quench all the fiery darts of the wicked. And take the helmet of salvation, and the sword of the Spirit, which is the word of God: Praying always with all prayer and supplication in the Spirit . . . .
>
> —Ephesians 6: 10-18a

You must ask the Lord to dress you with His armor. The Scripture asks that we put on the whole armor of God. Look at the soldiers. They will not enter a battle without wearing their armor. The same way, as God's children, we must ask Him to dress us with His armor for war.

CHAPTER 16

Intercessors' call

Many years ago when I lived in New York I attended the YMCA at least three times a week, to keep up with my physical exercise. Every year, the church goes on a 21-day fast. It included being in the church 6 a.m. and 6 p.m. for one-hour every day for 21 days. After the 6 a.m. prayer I spent some time at the YMCA before going home. One morning I was on the treadmill and had a fainting spell. I got off and sat down. The young man on the other treadmill got off and prayed with me. I had no idea who he was. However, I felt better and resumed my exercise on the treadmill. The brother began to question me about my ministry.

"What's your calling?" He asks.

"I am a missionary, an evangelist." I replied.

"I don't care who you say you are, the Lord has made you an intercessor, and He wants to know that He can trust you. In other words, if you see your pastor with another woman, don't talk about it but pray. You may talk to the pastor, but don't tell anybody else. All the other gifts come under that." He explained. He went on to say, "As an intercessor you have to be careful because God has blessed intercessors with wisdom, sometimes they feel nobody could talk to them." After that lecture I found out that this young man was a pastor whose church was located in the neighborhood.

Now my ministry became clearer to me. I would wake up at the wee hours of the morning with someone on my mind and realize the Lord wants me to pray for that person. Many years prior to that, I would wake up at nights and couldn't go back to sleep. I didn't realize it was a time to pray until much later as I grew in the Lord. At one time I felt that God was keeping me too occupied even when I had a great need to sleep. It is all being made clear to me today. I thank Him for teaching me how to pray. Now I can see the great need for intercessory prayer at this time. Since then, prayer has become part of my life. If it were not for prayer I would most certainly not be on this side of heaven. I thank God for pushing and letting me know the importance of staying at His feet.

Today, nobody wants to pray. I heard a minister say in her preaching many years ago, "Nobody hangs around the altar anymore. They are concerned with the food they left on the stove, or where they are going to eat. She said, I remember we would be at the altar praying and mother would roll and I would roll behind her." Of course no one has this kind of passion for spending time at the altar these days.

At this end time when the nation is in trouble, the focus is on the news, and the economic situation. But prayer must take priority in the lives of the church and the individual in the home. When the Lord encouraged me to get on with this assignment, I realized hell could not stop the vision. And all the demons that come against me today cannot stop it. The Lord will see to that. When I think of what God has in store for me I have no time to look at what the devil is trying to do. I cannot be defeated because God has me in the palm of His hand. In fact, a few years ago He gave me a word straight from the Scripture. It reads: "Behold, I have graven you upon the palms of my hands . . ." (Isaiah 49:16a). So, the enemy is fighting a losing battle.

Power in the written Word

For years I have been facing hell, but none of its fire was able to consume me because there is a higher power to which no devil can measure up. You can rest in the fact that God will see you through even if you are in the valley of the shadow of death. We have to go through the valley prior to experiencing the mountain top. Let us not make the mistake of thinking we can be on the mountain without having an encounter with the valley experience. It is part of the territory—part of the Christian life.

As I mentioned earlier, the devil tried tempting Jesus during His vulnerable moment, a time of fasting and prayer. The Scripture tells us that Jesus fought back with the written Word and said, "It is written, man shall not live by bread alone but by every word that proceeds out of the mouth of God" (Luke 4:1-11; Matthew 4: 1-10). The Lord brought this word to my attention years ago in a dream. The Lord handed me a note. It read, Luke 4: 1-11. I realized the Lord was warning me of the impending attacks, but that my strength would come from the Word of God. The Scripture also admonishes us, "Let us therefore come boldly unto the throne of grace, that we may obtain mercy, and find grace to help in time of need" (Hebrews 4:16). We have the privilege of going directly behind the veil to worship the true and living God. He loved us so much that "He gave His only begotten son, that whosoever believes in Him should not perish but have everlasting life" (John 3:16). Scripture also says, "For we have not an high priest who cannot be touched with the feeling of our infirmities; but was in all points tempted like as we are, yet without sin" (Hebrews 4:15). Here we are reminded that the Lord Jesus understands where we are because He, too, went through great trials and persecution here on earth. In Him we have an example that we, too, will experience much suffering. Yet, have no fear and don't give up. All strength comes from God. He is never too busy to listen to you. Friends will disappoint you but God is always ready with outstretched arms to receive and embrace you. What an honor and a privilege to be able to call on Him at any time, in the wee hours of the morning, at midnight and during the day.

Determination

The Scripture speaks of a certain woman who had an issue of blood twelve years. She tried many physicians, spent all she had and nothing worked for her. But one day she heard about Jesus. She joined the crowd and touched Him by faith. For she said, "If I may touch his clothes, I shall be whole." And immediately she was healed of that plague. (Mark 5:25-34). This woman was determined to receive her healing. To do so, she must come in touch with Jesus personally. Because of her insistence and faith, the Lord Jesus healed her. Your faith can disrupt some stuff. The Scripture says, "Trust in the Lord with all your heart . . . ." (Proverbs 3: 5-6). Faith is defined in the Scripture as, "The substance of things hoped for, the evidence of things not seen" (Hebrews 11:1). This means, believe God with all your heart despite your circumstances. Pastor Franklin has a beautiful example of faith. He puts it this way, "Living in the faith zone means reaching up and grabbing hold of nothing and holding on to it until it becomes something." With all the references and suggestions, I love this one.

Even in the midst of my turmoil God is handing me dreams on a platter. The dreams are so many that my large notebook is almost full of those nuggets from the Lord. So God is a great encourager. Even if your life is messed up—even when your life does not depict the plan of God for your life, God reminds you that He is not far off. Often, one is held captive by intimidation, what would this person say, what would the church say? All these traditions can keep you bound. But thank God for His mercy.

The apostle Paul encouraged his spiritual son, Timothy, to "stir up the gift of God," "For God has not given you a spirit of fear, but of power, and of love and of a sound mind" (2 Timothy 1:7). You always need a mentor to encourage you. The apostle Paul was a true mentor, we can learn so much from his example in the Word of God. His character was one of encouragement. Obviously, the apostle was aware of something in Timothy's life that needed to shift into another gear. He had to stir up the gift that was lying dormant for whatever reason. Many of us can relate to that. The gifts are always there but we need to shake it up and put it to use.

Obstruction

Even when you are wondering in your mind why things are not going the way they should, the Lord is faithful to let you know where the obstacle lies. In my prayer many months ago, the Lord whispered the word—"Sanballat." I mentioned this before, but I would like to give you a detailed account of this. After meditating on this name for a while, I opened my Bible to the book of Nehemiah and read some of the passages, particularly Nehemiah Chapter Four. It explains how Sanballat and Tobiah did everything in their power to hinder the work of God as Nehemiah built the wall of Jerusalem. This tells me that the adversary will try anything in its power to stop your progress.

Nehemiah is an example of a praying leader, a Biblical model of a godly leader in government, a man of wisdom, principle, courage, impeccable integrity, unwavering faith, compassion for the oppressed and great gifts in leadership and organization. Throughout his years as governor, Nehemiah remained righteous, humble, free from greed, self-sacrificing and uncorrupted by his prominence or power. He is one of the foremost Old Testament examples of a praying leader (also Daniel). No less than eleven times he is described as addressing God in prayer or intercession. He was a man who accomplished seemingly impossible tasks because of his complete trust in God.

The book graphically illustrates that prayer, sacrifice, hard work and tenacity, go together in realizing a God-given vision. Sanballat tried his utmost to stop Nehemiah's progress but in vain. In the same way, if you remain faithful God will warn you that a devious individual is hanging around your territory looking to trip you. The swindler might come with enticing words of greetings, but depending on where you are in Christ you will know that the crooks are set out to hinder your progress.

The attacks were coming at me, but I didn't know the extent and the location from which they were coming. However, the Lord gave me a strategy by bringing that name to my attention, so that I may know how and what direction to take during my prayer session. God is marvelous indeed. Who can stand in His way? In fact, who can stand in your way when God is watching over you? When God is for you who can be against you?

Just to give you an idea what was happening in Nehemiah's day. He received news that the exiles who returned to Judah from Babylon and Persia were in trouble and the wall of Jerusalem were still in shambles. After weeping, praying and fasting about Jerusalem's plight, Nehemiah was providentially authorized by the king to go to Jerusalem to serve as governor and to rebuild the city walls. As an inspired leader, he rallied his countrymen to rebuild the wall completely in only 52 days despite serious and determined opposition from inside and outside the city.

While serving the king, Nehemiah was known to be a man of prayer. Like the prophet Daniel, Nehemiah does not hide the fact that he serves a great and Mighty God by putting Him first in prayer. He was a man who accomplished seemingly impossible tasks because of his complete dependence on God. He knew that all these must go together in realizing a God-given vision. His first impulse was to pray. The Scripture says to us, "Pray without ceasing" (1 Thessalonians (5:17). So that when the occasion arises, you don't have to give God a historical background on what's taking place in your life at that moment. At times Nehemiah had to breathe a prayer to God for wisdom before answering the king's question. Sometimes he could only cry out to God from his heart.

Only after studying Nehemiah's encounter with the enemy, I realized why God brought the name 'Sanballat' to my attention. He was letting me know that the enemy was out to stop me, and in order to accomplish this task, prayer must take priority, mixed with hard work. In other words, pray and continue working. Don't give up.

All we know in Scripture about the enemy, Sanballat, is that he had apparently some civil or military command in Samaria, in the service of king Artaxarxes, and that from the moment of Nehemiah's arrival in Judea, he set himself to oppose every measure for the welfare of Jerusalem, and was a constant adversary of the Persian governor of Judah, borne by Nehemiah. According to the Scripture, his companions in this hostility were Tobiah the Ammonite, and Geshem the Arab. (Neh. 2:19; 4:7)

Why did God whisper to me "Sanballat?" You who are doing business with God need to take hold of this and know that the adversary will try to hinder your progress. Yet, if you are faithful to God, He will be faithful to you, and show you that an enemy is lurking around with the intention of blocking your progress. The Scriptures explain in Nehemiah that when Sanballat and his followers heard of Nehemiah's attempt to build, they began to move against him to obstruct the work. This encouraged Nehemiah to build quickly, and that disturbed the enemy who became very angry and began to mock the Jews, accusing them of being feeble. In fact, they said, "what are these feeble Jews doing?" Tobiah mocked, "Even a fox can break down their stone wall" (Neh.4:3). They threatened to kill the workers and because of the dangerous threat of Sanballat, the builders prayed to God "and set a watch against them day and night" (Neh. 4:9). The builders needed encouragement and Nehemiah was there for them. His words to them were, "don't be afraid of them, remember the Lord, who is great and terrible and fight for you, your brethren, your sons and your daughters, your wives and your houses" (v.14). "Our God shall fight for us" (v. 20).

Sanballat and his house were not giving up. They insisted on stopping God's work and sent messages to Nehemiah several times asking him for an audience. "Come let's talk." They asked. Full of wisdom, Nehemiah knew that was intended for evil. So his answer was, "I am doing a great work, I can't come down; why should the work cease while I leave it and come down to you?" (Neh. 5:3). The opposition continued to send messages, to no avail. In desperation, realizing God had accomplished the work Sanballat is making his final plea by creating false accusation against Nehemiah. Isn't this familiar?

When the enemy realizes that God is on your side, his last hope is to bring all kinds of false accusation against you. However, the Scripture tells us that the battle is God's. The enemy's bombardment must be broken because the battle is God's. I will not throw in the towel. By now the enemy ought to know he is fighting a losing battle. He must leave God's people alone. I am bought with a price, paid with blood—the precious blood of Jesus.

Intercessors have a heavenly connection with Jesus Christ and all those who are trying out God's people need to layoff. They cannot win, because God is watching over His children. Of course, faithfulness to God does not guarantee believers' freedom from suffering. In fact, Jesus taught that we are to expect it. "They shall put you out of the synagogues: the time comes that whosoever kills you will think he does God service" (John 16:2). And Paul's instruction to Timothy reads, "All who will live godly in Christ Jesus shall suffer persecution" (2Tim:3:12).

The Bible provides numerous examples of Godly people who experienced a significant amount of suffering for a variety of reasons. For example, because of jealousy by his brothers, Joseph was targeted for evil. Because of the jealousy of King Saul, David was targeted for evil. Scripture tells us in Job Chapter One that Job was a perfect and upright man. In fact, God said to Satan, "Have you considered my servant job, that there is none like him in the earth, a perfect and an upright man, one who respects God and shuns evil?" (Job 1:8). Yet Satan targeted Job by inflicting all manner of evil on him and his household. Satan reply was, "Does Job respect God for nothing? You have him and his house well protected, and have blessed the work of his hands, and increased his goods" (Job 1:10).

In his book you have the history of Job's sufferings, and his patience under them, but not without a mixture of human frailty. The book gives a biographical description of a man who loses everything—his wealth, family and health. It revolves around the perplexing question of why the righteous suffer, and how their suffering can be reconciled with the goodness and holiness of God. The traditional Jewish explanation was that all suffering was due to sin. The focus ought to be on what Job learns from his suffering, that God is sovereign over all creation.

The book raises questions and problems which are answered perfectly in Christ who identifies with our sufferings. As a High Priest, Jesus felt similar pain. As a result, He can relate to us. "For we have not a high priest who cannot be touched with the feeling of our infirmities . . ." (Hebrews 4:15). Many Bible characters, both in the Old and the New Testament can attest to the fact that suffering comes with the territory.

For example, God understood, and sympathized with Job's suffering, and weighed his words and feelings with compassion. God's speeches dealt entirely with the natural world of creation and nature such as, "Where were you when I laid the foundation of the earth." He would let Job know that He was always there even when Job questioned the where about of God during his suffering. Isn't that what we think at times when we are going through? The prophet Habakkuk had the same dilemma. God, where are you when all this wickedness is taking place, what are you doing about it? Well, God's reply shocked him. God let him know that He will send the Chaldeans to take care of the problem. The Chaldeans are wicked people, yet God is using them to trash out the situation that's taking place with the present enemies. The Prophet Habakkuk could not understand why God would use a people who were more vicious, to correct the situation. However, the prophet soon learns that it is up to God to decide the kind of punishment.

Also, in His conversation with Job, God described the mystery and complexity of the universe, and revealed that His method of ruling the world is far beyond our ability to comprehend. God wanted Job to understand that His activity in the world of nature is similar to his rule in the moral and spiritual order to the universe, and that complete understanding of God's ways will never be found in this life.

The Book of Job does reveal that when all truth is finally known, God's ways and actions will be seen as just and righteous. Also, God reassured him of the most important thing, He had not abandoned him. The Lord was there watching over him constantly. And so He is the same today always watching over us. What can we learn from this testimony? Many of you might consider yourself in a real battle—going through trials, suffering financially, and experiencing health challenges. I can assure you God is right where you are. I feel Him even when I am going through hell. He lets me know He is there by sharing light on His Word. He whispers a song in my spirit. The next time He gives me a Word from the Bible. He knows the steps that you take, and has a plan for your life. He declares in Scripture, "For I know the plans that I have for you, 'declares the Lord,' plans for welfare and not for calamity to give you a future and a hope" (Jeremiah 29:11 NASB). If you are going through the fire and the Lord Jesus is not in the center of your life, you will find it extremely difficult to make it through the flame. However, when you have a relationship with Him, you are able to cope with any situation with patience. There is no case too difficult for God to fix. He can change your situation and deliver you from the wickedness of men, even from your abusive situation, so that you can testify of His goodness.

God has a great purpose for your life. Hold on to Him and don't give up. There is hope in Jesus Christ. When your back is against the wall you can stand flat-footed and say, 'I know in whom I have believed and he is able to deliver me whatever the circumstances.' He is the God who left His Divinity, took on humanity through a virgin birth, to demonstrate to us His understanding of what it means to suffer persecution. He went through terrible trials, and can feel our pain. He is very sympathetic toward your situation, even your abusive marriage. I have proved Him over and over. Just imagine you are working in the kingdom, but deep down in your spirit you sense a hindrance by the forces of evil, then God shows up with a ready-made word—a revelation, "Sanballat." God is awesome! I love Him with all my heart.

CHAPTER 17

Culture differentiation in marriage

In some culture, if you marry someone against your parents' wishes you are setting yourself up for disaster. In the event their choice does not meet your approval you simply have to work at it. Marriage is hard work. The easiest part is the wedding ceremony. Love is strange because love is more than the flutter of the heart. It's a commitment that will force you to include the Lord Jesus in the relationship, because it is not an easy task. Don't do it alone just because you have the romantic feeling. It all seems perfect at the time, only to find you had a raw deal.

In an article concerning marriage, the conversation was based on married women who never once heard the words "I'm sorry" from their husbands. Some men find it difficult to say, "I'm sorry." However, these same men will often do something nice that says "I'm sorry" in a different way. They might bring home your favorite ice cream, or buy you a bunch of flowers on Valentine's Day or a book you wanted for a long time. Some people don't know any other way to say "I'm sorry." If others are sorry for something they have done to you in the past, you should rejoice and be grateful. I had many "I'm sorry" moments from my spouse and those have been always temporary until the abuse began again. All the "I'm sorry" went out the window at that point. So what's the purpose? Sorry today, and tomorrow he is demonstrating his gruesome behavior. I will take the flowers or some other gesture anytime, rather than have the "I'm sorry" moments if it is only temporarily. Where there is no physical abuse, I'll favor these individuals anytime over the one who constantly says "I'm sorry" but refuses to seek council.

God's love confronts all evil

God loved us so much, that despite our wretchedness He forgives with no hesitation. He doesn't push you to get right before He forgives you. He expects you to say 'I'm sorry' when the occasion arises. My spouse did not have a problem saying "I'm sorry." That was the reason for my holding out and tolerating the abuse for such a long time. That is why I bore the shame for as long as I did. However, living with such an individual who was sorry one minute and became abusive the same day was quite challenging too. I felt he was going to be crying over my grave saying, "I'm sorry." I thought of that even when he came to my door and requested that we join in matrimony a second time. Won't you feel sorry for someone like that who, despite the mental derangement, will not seek treatment? How long is this going to go on? There comes a time when one has to find an escape route or end up in the grave.

Relocation did not stop the attacks

At last I found that escape route, only to find that my problems were just about to begin. I was set to prepare for war at a time when I had no idea how to war. I was not aware of the documented facts in the Scriptures. Yes, the Bible is replete with information concerning your whole life. However, things were happening in my life and had no idea from where they were coming, and from whom they were coming until the Lord revealed it to me. Those fiery darts kept coming, attacking my finances, attacking me on every side. The only prayer in my vocabulary was what's documented in the church missal, or mass book, or what I learned from my grandmother. That was my background and thought at the time that was a good background to have.

Grandmother woke all the grandchildren every morning at 4:00 a.m. to say the Rosary. Today, when I look back from where I came, I thank God for His mercy, for the Scripture says, "O give thanks unto the Lord; for he is good: for his mercy endures forever" (Psalm 136:1). Yes, He is a wonderful, merciful Father on whom we can call at any time, even at the wee hours of the morning. As a child, I got an education in rising early to pray, and walking five miles to the Cathedral for 5:00 a.m. novena services. Today, as born again Christians we realize the importance of praying the Word from Scriptures. Now I can appreciate the wonderful grace of God. A few weeks ago, because of what I have been going through, I had a serious conversation with the Lord before going to bed. On waking He gave me a revelation from His Word: "For by grace you are saved through faith; and that not of yourselves: it is the gift of God" (Ephesians 2:8). I got up from bed, got hold of my Bible and read that Scripture over and over, meditated on it for at least thirty minutes. Then I concluded that, despite what I am going through God wants me to know that He is aware of my struggle, and that His grace is sufficient to keep me.

There are, no doubt, many problems in your life today, and there will be many problems for those who do business with God. It comes with the territory. Consider what Jesus went through for you and me and how He handled every demonic force that came against Him. It is all written in the Bible. You must remove all surface issues if the plan God has for you is to materialize. I can assure you that He has placed seeds of greatness within you, but if those seeds are constantly consumed with weeds, they will not develop. I realize we must tap into God's favor, yield to it, and let that greatness come forth.

Today, in the uncertainty of the world's unrest, we have the opportunity to enjoy Jesus Christ and all the gifts God has given us. Just receive it. Remove those things that so easily offend you and grab hold of the tremendous blessings God has instilled in you, and work it. Yes, just work it! Move forward with that vision. Don't let it die. The warfare is in the mind. Consequently, the Scripture says: "Be not conformed to this world: but be transformed by the renewing of your mind . . ." (Romans 12:2a). This means, we have to keep our minds saturated with the Word of God, because Satan uses the spirit of deception to control the mind. We ought to apply the blood of Jesus on our situation and read the Word of God daily, in order to ward off the forces of evil. Reading the Word on a daily basis has become part of my life. I suggest everyone do likewise. Use the Word and apply the blood of Jesus on your situation; then believe the Lord for victory as you live in an atmosphere of praise and worship.

Just think about this, while you are going through hell in your home, the Lord has already prepared a place in glory for you to enjoy. He says, "Let us come boldly to the throne of grace to obtain mercy and find grace to help in the time of need" (Hebrews 4:16). We don't have to go through a third person. God has given us the authority to come directly to Him.

As I began to experience a new place in God, I found the true essence of His glory by studying the Bible with eagerness. I learned that when God calls you to a place in Him, He is simply saying in order to come up higher you need to take a stand and study 'My Word.' I find it refreshing as it gets deep down in my soul. For example, the Scripture says, "Study to show yourself approved unto God, a workman that need not be ashamed, rightly dividing the word of truth" (2 timothy 2:15). The Greek word for study means to be eager, be diligent. We have to work the Word. Our maturing is based on the Word. It trains us in righteousness. The Word is able to cut deeply into our life for every good work. I have tried and found it invaluable. Nothing else can surpass the Word of God when you are going through the valley of decision. Glory to God!

Praise and worship can set the atmosphere for entering into God's presence. To worship God in the glory is to present your body a living sacrifice, holy and acceptable in His sight. Here, the anointing will take you to another realm in the glory.

The Lord ministered to me many months ago and requested that I remove from this earthly realm unto a higher level in Him. In this vision, God gave me the opportunity to see myself standing on the earth and looking up at a mountain. As a result, I find myself praying differently, with a better understanding of where the Lord is taking me. Some people wouldn't understand where you are coming from, and sometimes feel threatened by your anointing. But when you are going through some dark days your prayer must reflect a place in God where He is shooting you out of your present situation into the glory realm, where you can linger in His anointing.

The Lord takes me through many passages in the Bible and has not stopped showing me His glory. I have to be careful not to fail Him by continually being disobedient. I have not always been able to carry out His assignments consistently. For example, I can accomplish one job at a time. Until I complete the writing assignment, I cannot seem to handle the music. Working at the piano takes much concentration and I need to spend more time in this capacity. However, I find myself moving slowly toward that end, and one day I will gain the victory at the piano with the help of God.

Maturing in God

Maturity in God begins with a childlike attitude and a humble spirit. The Scripture says, "Verily I say unto you, except you be converted, and become as little children, you shall not enter into the kingdom of heaven" (Matthew 18:3). When Jesus used the word 'little' as an example of humbling ourselves, He was indicating that as adults we have to be teachable. This can only manifest itself by becoming as little children . . . Humility comes with a teachable spirit and a willingness to trust God. For example, we ought to do what God commands without questioning Him. Children are free of malice and prejudice. Doubtful questioning is not in their vocabulary; hence the reason the Lord used them to demonstrate his purpose. Many of us want to wait until we understand everything before starting on the pathway of the kingdom. That was my plight until I received clarity. Begin to obey, and the rest of the vision will come. God will come forth when you least expect Him.

Salvation a requirement

Theologically, before we begin to mature in God, it is necessary to become converted. This does not denote merely a single act of sorrow or penitence. It is embracing an attitude of abundant life. There must be a Godly sorrow, a genuine sorrow for sin that leads to repentance. For example, a change of heart will cause you to turn from sin to God; that leads to salvation. Repentance from sin and faith in Jesus Christ are human responsibilities in salvation. Jesus says, "Repent for the kingdom of heaven is at hand" (Matthew 3:2). In contrast, the unrepentant often become sorry only for the consequences of their sin but will not change the life of sinning. Such sorrow results in eternal death and judgment. For the Scripture says, ". . . The wages of sin is death; but the gift of God is eternal life through Jesus Christ our Lord" (Romans 6:23). Believe in the Lord Jesus and you shall be saved. It is by faith.

When Jesus spoke to the woman with the issue of blood who desired to touch the hem of His garment, He said: "Daughter, your faith has made you whole; go in peace, and be healed of your plague" (Mark 5:34). It was possible that her healing would not happen if she had not moved in faith. She was determined this was her time to receive her miracle, and the Lord granted her request because she believed in Him. Glory to His name!

As you begin to see signs and wonders however small at the time, know that God has much more in store for you. Obey Him in the small things, and greater opportunity will come. Gradually He will take you to a new place in Him. God has things for you that you cannot even fathom. Don't worry about the lack of understanding. He is ready to move in your life despite your flaws. You might be the least in the eyes of others, but you are set for great things if you stay with Jesus and bathe in the Word of God. Just be obedient. As the apostle Paul declares, you are "born out of due season"—out of time.

Jesus came to set the captives free. Yet we seem to remain captivated by the enemy. The Lord has given us the authority over these demonic forces. To reiterate, He tells us in the Scripture: "I have given you power to tread on serpents and scorpions, and over all the power of the enemy; and nothing shall by any means hurt you" (Luke 10:19). The Greek terminology for this power is "Dunamais." It means authority—powerful. This authority is in the name of Jesus. This power belongs to God's children. We are free to use it, free to take up our position in Christ Jesus. We ought to know who we are and whose we are. The Word of God says: "Before I formed you in the belly I knew you, and before you came forth out of the womb I sanctified you and I ordained you a prophet unto the nations" (Jeremiah 1:5). He says in the book of Romans, "Whom He predestined, these He also called; and whom he called, these He also justified; and whom He justified, these he also glorified" (Romans 8:30 NASB). Therefore, it's already settled in the mind of God where He plans to take you. Who can stand in your way when God has ordained you for the work of the ministry? As long as you are in Him no one could stop you. Stay focused on His Word. I appreciate the word in the book of Timothy.

The Scripture says he was appointed a preacher, and an apostle, and a teacher of the Gentiles. For this cause he suffered much persecution. He said, "nevertheless I am not ashamed: for I know whom I have believed, and I am persuaded that he (God) is able to keep that which I have committed unto him against that day" (2 Timothy 1:12). Timothy knew that the God whom he believed and trusted and relied on is able to guard and keep that which has been entrusted to him, and which he has committed to God until that day. The idea is that "God has not given us a spirit of fear; but of power, and of love, and of a sound mind" (2 Timothy 1:7). God has given us a mind to think clearly despite the enemy's bombardment. The Scripture says, He has called us "with a holy calling, not according to our works, but according to his own purpose and grace, which was given us in Christ Jesus before the world began" (2 Timothy 1:9). The apostle Paul encouraged Timothy to stir up the gift. The Greek word for "gift" is charisma. It must have been a special anointing from the Holy Spirit to fulfill his ministry. The gifts and power bestowed on you by the Holy Spirit do not automatically remain strong. They must be fueled by the grace of God through your prayer, faith, obedience and diligence. You must stir it up. Pray without ceasing, put on faith and move out with boldness.

Diligence in our ministry

Diligence is important because we can get caught up in ministry while focusing on ourselves and not having God at the center of what we are doing. For example, I enjoyed taking a meal to the clients in one of New York City's shelters during the summer months. As a church group we provided this outside. At other times we did this by appointment after their evening service. The clients always looked forward to this kind of food. However, I was bothered by the fact that we were serving these people without ministering to them spiritually. My feeling about what I was doing was getting in the way of sharing the Good News. Others were doing it for the same reason. We were doing this, but had lost track of God's purpose, to minister salvation to His people.

The real reason for ministering to one's physical needs should be to share the Gospel of Jesus Christ. This was exactly Jesus' intention when He fed the multitude before sharing the Gospel with them. Jesus Christ looked at the thousands who followed Him and felt love and compassion for them. He knew they were hungry and tired, and realized the only way to hold their attention was to provide physical food before ministering to them spiritually. (John 6: 5-12)

After realizing what we were doing, we changed our motive and invited the participants to Jesus. At other times I was concerned about preaching on the roadside in the same area, without dealing with them on a personal level. Everyone has special needs. Many years ago the Lord placed in my heart, during my street ministry, the need to minister to the people on a personal level. As a result, I invited a sister to join me, and it was surprising to see how receptive those individuals were as we walked and talked and ministered to them individually.

Some unfortunate situations

Sometimes I see a young man in the shelter whose demeanor does not seem to warrant his being there. So I would ask, "Why are you here?" His reply was: "I had some bad luck, so I'm here temporarily until I get myself together." Here was a perfect opportunity to share the Gospel with him. Others found being in the shelter a horrible experience because of the way they were treated by their fellow inhabitants. And then there were others who knew the Lord, but circumstances beyond their control caused them to be at the shelter. For many of those individuals it was a temporary situation, and so we needed to pray that God would get them out of that situation in due time. These are the kind of situations we need to pray about today. It is amazing to discover the various kinds of people in these shelters who, for different reasons, found themselves there in line to receive a plate of hot home-style food, because the shelter did not offer them what they had hoped for in terms of food.

Despite all this, spiritual burn-out is real. No matter how much we enjoy serving in a ministry, being in good health is critical. It is easy to become mentally and physically fatigued, and so we need wisdom as we minister to people. We cannot serve effectively with a worn out body, certainly not with a broken down mentality. Good health includes attitudes that are conducive to kingdom business, such as walking in love and forgiveness. The Lord is full of surprises and we have to be ready for these sudden nudges from Him, even in the midst of our busy schedules.

CHAPTER 18

God is full of surprises

Probably because of tradition, prisoners are looked upon as castaways. They are the outcast, unloved members of the family, and the church sometimes treats them as such. But according to the Scriptures, Jesus indicates that showing compassion to those who are hungry, thirsty or imprisoned is showing compassion to Him. (Matthew 25: 31-46). Because we are all one in the body of Christ, He also says, "Remember those in prison as if you were their fellow prisoners, and who are mistreated as if you yourselves were suffering" (Hebrews 13:3). Many years ago, because of a dream that I had, I became concerned about prison ministry. In the dream I found myself preaching at the prison gate to a large audience, including one of my brothers. In the dream he was incarcerated for drugs. The dream was so real I couldn't get it out of my mind.

As I began to meditate on the dream, the Lord gave me clarity many months later. Operating in the "word of knowledge" a young pastor revealed to me that the Lord had made me an intercessor. I already cited this. Later the Holy Spirit reminded me that interceding for those who are incarcerated is part of my ministry. I began praying specifically for inmates and their families. After praying intensely for a season, I began interceding occasionally. It's amazing how God speaks to you in dreams and visions, and after many years you come to understand the meaning of the message as it unfolds right before your eyes. See how God is awesome. Let me tell you how this unfolding took place.

God is awesome

In August 1999, I traveled to Grenada to care for my mother. Before returning to New York I made a phone call to my cousin. The person answered: "Richmond Hill Prison."

"Sorry, wrong number, what number is this?" I asked.

I redialed the number and announced, "My name is Mary Johnson, an Evangelist visiting from New York, and would like to minister to the inmates before going back to New York."

With an appointment, I visited the prison. The Holy Spirit took over the ministry as the inmates played the guitar and other instruments, worshipping the Lord. Before I ministered, I requested that they sing something pertaining to the Holy Spirit. They were a blessing to me. Those men were prison inmates incarcerated for their involvement in the revolutionary battle on the Island of Grenada, resulting in a number of deaths, including the Prime Minister, Maurice Bishop. Consequently, I made this my regular assignment whenever I visited Grenada. Some of those men were well learned and one, an educator, teaching social science in the prison. They have a music ministry, and my first impression was, "Where are the inmates?" But they were the inmates. They were very receptive, and the Holy Spirit worked so mightily that I began to weep in their presence. I couldn't get anyone to accompany me to the prison for the first time. Nonetheless, it is good to know God is not 'a God of routine' or 'every day the same.' He works with you according to your ability and purpose.

Except when I was arrested and got a taste of what it was to be a pending inmate, this day for the first time, I was visiting the prison as kingdom business—to minister to inmates. I had no idea what I was going to say, but the Lord made a way and placed the words in my mouth. The Holy Spirit moved in such a mighty way and did the work. He ministered through me, in the name of Jesus. I asked the leader of the group, the social science instructor, "Is it usual that one person comes to minister in the prison?"

"No, many church groups come by appointments. Also, an ex-inmate comes back to minister to us." He said.

I left with a sense of gratitude, and praised God for allowing this. He worked it out so miraculously. I praised Him along the way, going home, and came back to America with joy unspeakable for the opportunity God gave me to minister to those thirteen men. They, too, looked forward to my visit. Since then I have been ministering to them at the prison whenever I go to Grenada. I just found out as I write that the inmates were released from prison, and the social scientist is now employed as a counselor to prison inmates. I am so happy for those brothers.

Their worship session in prison reminded me of the apostles Paul and Silas worshipping in the jail cell 2000 years ago, despite their unjust punishment. They were imprisoned for preaching the Gospel of Jesus Christ. While in prison they chose not to complain. Instead, they sang and praised God. Worship will give you victory every time. Even today, the church that fails to worship God will always experience spiritual dullness in the ministry.

I hope the inmates who were released will find proper employment or something substantial to keep their mind occupied. Of course these men were not from the streets, they were in the army where all the uproar began. Now they are back home and I wish them success in their new endeavor. Believe me if you can become a worshipper and forget all the problems facing you, God will give you a breakthrough. That was what I envisioned for those young men. God came through for them. Amen.

Reason for inmates returning to prison

Many years ago, I obtained a Bachelor's degree in Sociology, with a minor in Economics. One of the requirements for the degree was a course called "Criminology." One of the words I learnt in that course was "Recidivism." The term is used for one who constantly returns to jail for the same crime. Usually, minority groups are in this category. It shows then, that those who were well established financially were able to get around the system, and escape serious penalty for crimes they committed. I realize this is the reason intercessory prayer is so vital for prison inmates. God will intervene in the lives of these individuals regardless of whether or not they are financially able to fend for themselves.

Among the other trips to Grenada and the various islands, Trinidad was a major project in my ministry, where a sister and I ministered to the school children on the streets during their lunch period. We had some difficulty getting them back to their classrooms because of the beautiful tracts we distributed to the group. We had some in our possession when the final bell rang, and could not get the children to return to their classrooms. We literally had to push them into the schoolyard. Wherever we found ourselves children were at the center of our lives on the mission field.

Also, we preached in the market place, ministered to the vagrants on the streets and in the park. On another occasion, in another setting, we fed the men and women at the shelter in Trinidad. To reiterate, a few years later another sister and I went back to Trinidad and held a vocational bible school for one week. Children were transported by bus and the number attended the program were 110. It was a blessing. Also, assisted by the community and church members we had a wonderful experience with the outdoor cooking on the Island, including a health fare. As nurses, we used our skills to minister to the people in the community.

Because I returned to Grenada frequently, the sharing of cooked meals became part of my ministry there. The brethren from local churches and I visited the home for retarded children and ministered in the "poor house" as it is called. As for preaching, I loved street ministry. This is where I learned to preach with no fear. It is a rewarding experience to preach on the streets in the Caribbean Islands, as the people were eager to stop and listen. After several ministry trips to Grenada, I decided to rest, only to hear from the Lord: "Go and peach the Birth of Christ." Without question I knew that it could not be Grenada. No, not again! But I was wrong.

Christmas was around the corner and the Lord interrupted my schedule and directed me to go back to Grenada and preach Jesus. He was born of a virgin, suffered and died. He rose from the dead, and is now seated on the throne making intercession for us, and that Christmas is not about shopping and exchanging gifts.

Rather, it is about loving each other. By assisting those who are suffering in various ways you are doing it unto Jesus Christ, the one who suffered and died to show His sincere love for mankind. He expects us to encourage those who are brokenhearted, especially the ones who don't know Jesus.

As a result, on Christmas day 1985, when everyone was enjoying and celebrating the birth of Christ in New York, I left for Grenada to preach the Good News—the Birth, Death and Resurrection of Jesus. Traveling alone did not deter me because the brethren in Grenada were very supportive. I returned to New York, blessed, having made myself available to hear from God and to follow His instructions.

Summary of my mission trips

My mission began on the streets of New York. In 1983, I began foreign missions starting in my hometown, Grenada. In 1986, I journeyed to Israel and Rome with a church group. Although street ministry was not part of the agenda, walking where Jesus walked was ample for me at the time. This mission was an educational experience. It was seeing the Bible come alive in real life. We visited Jerusalem and the various sites where Jesus ministered; also, the Via Delarosa, where Jesus walked carrying the cross to Calvary. I was amazed to see a tree of thorns really existed in Jerusalem. I couldn't imagine those long spikes placed on Jesus' head. Oh, what wickedness! Just imagine the pain caused by that deep wound in His head. The blood comes flowing from the Master's head and down His face blocking His vision. Another area was the Garden of Gethsemane where Jesus knelt and prayed and sweated blood before His arrest, the Mount of Transfiguration where Jesus transformed Himself in the presence of His disciples—Peter, James and John; the upper room where the disciples tarried and waited for the anointing of the Holy Spirit, the Sea of Galilee and much more, was an education in itself.

In 1988, a world tour with Calvary Pentecostal Tabernacle took me to India, China, Asia, the Philippines and Hong Kong. We all had a chance to minister in the Philippines and in the streets of India. Our final stop was Hong Kong, very commercialized, like the western world. This ministry was associated with a home for retarded children in Asia. We were able to help in that ministry while we were there.

Throughout the 1990's I ministered in the Caribbean Islands, including St. Vincent, Trinidad and Tobago, Jamaica, repeated visits to Grenada and Trinidad. Finally, Bolivia, South America was my final trips in that section of the world.

In 2003 I returned to Israel and Egypt with Calvary Pentecostal Tabernacle where my experience was somewhat different. Also, the atmosphere was different. Terrorism was at its height. But we had experienced guides who manned the security so that we were quite safe during our stay there. I am grateful to God who gave me such wonderful opportunity to experience those places. In addition to reading the Scriptures, I have a much better understanding of whom Jesus really is and what He means to me simply by making that trip.

In the Garden, I experienced healing in my body when I knelt and laid my head on the stone on which Jesus leaned, as He prayed in the Garden of Gethsemane over 2000 years ago. While I was getting comfortable my team beckoned me to come along as they were ready to leave. I sensed something beautiful took place in me at that site. Something wonderful happened while resting on that stone. Hallelujah.

Jesus says in the Gospel, "At that day you shall know that I am in my Father and you in me, and I in you" (John 14:20). Jesus is saying here, we are in Him and He is in us. I sensed that oneness at the Garden. What an honor and a privilege to know that we are one in Him. It's a joy to know Him as Lord. It's a blessing to know Him as a friend, a friend that sticks closer than a brother. His name is the Lord Jesus, lover of my soul, Rose of Sharon, Lilly of the valley, the bright morning star, Almighty God. I love Him. When things look grim He encourages me with a word. When things seem hopeless He gives me a song. He often places a song in my heart. He gives me a song in the night; He gives me a song in the day, even in the midst of a storm He gives me a song.

CHAPTER 19

Excitement in the air

Missions are not without trials, but the outcome is rewarding, just to be able to help a nation or just one person. It is impossible to grow spiritually without trials. A few years ago, on one of my missionary journeys, I encountered what seemed to be my final bout, my last trip to the mission field and my flight to glory. But the Lord revealed to me that He was not ready for me on the other side of the planet. The plane had given a signal that danger was ahead, but it happened so suddenly; even while the flight attendants were in the isle serving lunch, the call came from the captain, "Flight attendants take your seats!" The sound of the plane was very distressing. It began to bounce back and forth and from side to side, and my traveling companion and I began to pray aloud. Included in the prayer was something I learned from the Word of God and was constantly put in effect by my pastor, Archbishop Wilbert McKinley, of the Elim International Fellowship. The Hebrew word for this is "Yaddah," and it means surrender praises to God with hands raised above your head. So here is my opportunity to Yaddah in public. I raised both hands and began to worship God, and thank and praise Him for safety. There are certain church folks who would be embarrassed by my action, because they will praise and worship God on the inside and shun Him on the outside, and might look at me as one who has lost her mind. But this was my time to prove God, even in public.

So I prayed continuously with my hands raised above my head. When all was quiet I lowered my hands and the Lord gave me a song. My missionary sister and I sang as I explained to her, "Sister, listen to the song the Lord has just given me." We both sang it while the words ministered to us. The song is this:

"God is still on the throne and He will remember His own,
Though trials oppress us and burdens distress us
He never will leave us alone,
God is still on the throne and He will remember His own,
His promise is true He will not forget you,
God is still on the throne."

—The Lord Jesus

God is awesome. To reiterate, He will give you a song in the night, He will give you a song in the day; even in the midst of a storm He will give you a song. Just be faithful. Of course this is how He ministers to me. This is the God I am talking about. He will come through for you when you least expect Him. He was in the beginning, as the Bible declares, "In the beginning was the Word and the Word was with God, and the Word was God. And the Word became flesh, and dwelt among us, and we beheld His glory, the glory as of the only begotten of the Father, full of grace and truth" (John 1:1, 14 NASB).

God is omnipotent—all powerful; He is omnipresent—He is here, there and everywhere at the same time. He is omniscience—an all knowing God. He is immutable—a God that cannot change. He cannot lie. His promise is true; He will never leave you nor forsake you. The ones who don't know Him personally are really missing a treat in their lives. His name is Jesus Christ, the Son of God. There is power in the name of Jesus. You can use His name with confidence and experience victory in your lives. He has given you the authority to do so. His name is invaluable on the mission field where the evil force resides in the homes and on the streets, whose mission is to hamper and destroy you.

Consequently, that trip was an experience for my traveling companion and me. It was her first missionary endeavor, and her first time coming with me to Grenada. Once we got to the Island, she demonstrated boldness, and was not afraid to approach anyone with whom we came in contact.

As ambassadors we are proud to be able to say God has sent us to preach the Gospel. The scientists and philosophers have a tough time believing in the virgin birth. Members of the Sanhedrin such as the Sadducees doubted the resurrection. To the Jews it's a stumbling block, to the Greeks it's foolishness; but to those who believe, it is the power of God unto salvation. We must get to the place where we believe that every Word in the Bible is "given by the inspiration of God and is profitable for doctrine, for reproof, for correction, for instruction in righteousness; that the man of God may be perfect, thoroughly furnished unto all good work" (2Tim. 3:16-17). Hence the reason one must be diligent in studying the Word of God. It is a privilege to know Him and accept Him as Lord of our lives. There is so much happening out there and people are looking for answers in the wrong places. Yet, God has supplied all those answers in the Word of God—the Bible. The Agnostics say that man's mind is too finite to know God, but the Bible is replete with evidence that lets us know God is knowable. Those who say otherwise are the ones who fail to spend time with God on a personal level. To know God you must fellowship with Him daily through the Word—the Logos. We are blessed to have free access to the Word.

Missionaries in foreign countries, who are going through trials and have limited access to the Bible, find themselves sharing a few pages with one another. They need our prayers and support. Here, in the Western world we are blessed to be able to read the Bible freely without reservation. On our missionary journey, it is such a rewarding experience to be able to share Bibles with others who are not fortunate to own a Bible of their own. Even without a Bible prayer must be a priority; because the adversary will do everything in its power to hinder your progress and God's work. The apostle Paul was going through much pain when he asked the Lord to remove the sting of injustice and misery. The Lord came back with an answer that many of us would look at as unfair. But when the Lord says, "My grace is sufficient to keep you," He is saying in essence I am here for you, I'll go through the valley with you, but that does not mean that I am going to remove the sting that comes with the journey as you go through your valley experience. You are not going to die but you are going to make it and come out like gold after going through the fire. The author of the book of Job puts it this way, "But he knows the way that I take: when he has tried me, I shall come forth as gold" (Job 23:10). In this Old Testament book, we observe that Job was experiencing much suffering, but was not hearing from God with whom he had good relationship. However, he was confident that in the midst of this trial, God was going to see him through. In the final analysis God came through for Job by restoring all that he had lost.

There are many other examples but one that stands out in my mind is found in the life of Joseph, the son of Jacob. Genesis chapters 37-50 gives us a picture of one who experienced joy and many blessings having gone through many struggles that led to imprisonment, a life of slavery, injustice, false accusation, and suffered violently at the hands of his brothers. But even in the midst of this, God had a plan for Joseph. A perfect example of a life that stands out as an encouragement to all who are going through trials, tragedies, problems in the homes and problems on the jobs. Joseph is a model of how God uses affliction to shape your character and prepare you for the call on your life. Joseph used his pain and trials to gain access into the kingdom of God. He had access to God's heart as he remained faithful to Him, despite his persecution.

An example of tolerance

Joseph was Jacob's favorite son by his favorite wife, Rachel. Jacob gave him a princely robe—a robe of many colors, which in ancient times represented the father's intention of bestowing on his son a double blessing. Every boy was dressed in a tunic, but Joseph tunic stood out as a princely garment. As a young boy Joseph had two dreams that revealed his ascent to a position of power and authority, and his future elevation over his brothers and family. Joseph made known the dreams to his brothers. As a result, they despised and set out to kill him.

They were finally persuaded to sell him to Israelite traders, who carried Joseph to Egypt and sold him into slavery. At this point things looked hopeless and it appeared as though those dreams would never materialize. Humanly speaking there was no possibility of Joseph even surviving his struggles. The odds were against him.

But God! If He gives you a promise, trust Him to fulfill that promise, and no devil in hell can stop it from materializing.

God prospered Joseph, and granted him favor in the eyes of Potiphar, one of Pharaoh's officers and captain of the palace guard. Potiphar made Joseph his personal servant and put him in charge of his household. But because Joseph was righteous and faithful to God he was unjustly thrown into prison, based on a false accusation by Potiphar's wife. Yet God blessed Joseph even in the midst of adversity. He was put in charge of the prisoners where he had the opportunity to interpret the dreams of two inmates, the king's cupbearer and his chief baker. Joseph reminded the cupbearer to keep him in mind when he was back in position, but the cupbearer forgot his promise to speak to the Pharaoh on Joseph's behalf. Yet during Joseph's time in prison, God was preparing him for something great. How was God doing that? Certainly not by pampering him; In fact, Joseph went through great trials on a daily basis.

God is so wonderful. He will bring dreams to pass in His own time and on His terms. Because He is now ready to release Joseph from prison to a high calling, God gave Pharaoh two dreams that neither the wise men nor the magicians could interpret. Now the cupbearer, remembers a man in the prison whose name is Joseph, who would be able to interpret Pharaoh's dreams. In interpreting the dream, Joseph warns Pharaoh of the seven years of plenty to be followed by seven years of famine. Impressed or elated with Joseph's wisdom and discernment, Pharaoh appointed Joseph second in command to himself and in charge over all Egypt. A number of us can relate to Joseph's sufferings.

One might ask, "What does all this have to do with missions?" Missionaries in Sudan, Indonesia, the Middle East, Asia and other parts of the world are being killed for the Gospel. Others live to testify of the goodness of God, who brought them through despite the persecution. I used Joseph as an example of a missionary who was put to the test. He had a promise from God, and it appeared that the promise was not going to materialize. Wherever he found himself the enemy showed his ugly head. Yet Joseph remained calm throughout the whole ordeal. Joseph had to endure those trials for 13 years before God elevated him to a position of honor. Many missionaries could relate to that experience when we are threatened with physical abuse and death. As Joseph, we can learn many lessons and prove ourselves by being faithful and holding on to the Word of God with patience, believing that God will deliver us in due season. We all need to take note of these experiences, learn from them and know that betrayal and injustice come with the territory. Joseph trusted God and remained faithful without getting angry and bitter.

Today, many individuals question God because they cannot see Him and cannot even sense His presence when they are going through trials and persecution. They ask, "Where is God when I need Him?" I cannot take the pain, enough is enough! But here is an example, the life of Joseph and other Old Testament prophets such as Jeremiah, Daniel, Noah and Job, is proven fact that we can persevere even in the midst of what appears to be a hopeless situation and a lost dream.

There is a reason why this is written in the Bible. It tells us we are not alone in this; the people of that day went through much unfairness, likewise those in Sudan, Indonesia, Somalia and other countries, and we can learn from their experiences by taking note of how they handled every trial with patience. The Scripture says, "Wait on the Lord, be of good courage, and he shall strengthen your heart" (Psalm 27:4). "Commit your way unto the Lord, trust also in him and he shall bring it to pass" (Psalm 37:5). Waiting includes patience, trust and obedience. While you are waiting remain faithful and carry out any assigned task for the kingdom.

Joseph proved that he was worthy of honor. Even when Jacob, his father, pronounced the blessings on the children before he died, he said: "Joseph is a fruitful bough, even a fruitful bough by a well; whose branches run over the wall. The archers have surely grieved him, and shot at him, and hated him: But his bow abode in strength, and the arms of his hands were made strong by the hands of the mighty God of Jacob" (Genesis 49:22-24).

In other words, as Joseph remained faithful to God and persevered to the bitter end without murmuring, he allowed God to use his pain and suffering to produce fruit. Joseph became fruitful, a tremendous blessing to his people. The blessing was beyond measure, and so it will be to you and me who remain true to God. In addition to promoting him, Pharaoh blessed him with a wife. From this union, Joseph had two sons. Manasseh was the first-born. According to Merrill Unger of Unger's Bible Dictionary, the name Manasseh means, "causing to forget." It is the name of the fourteenth king of Judah and other biblical persons. Joseph said, regarding Manasseh: "for God has made me forget all my toil, and my father's house." (Genesis 41: 51). This is the result of every faithful missionary and or believer. Just hold on to the truth and God will see you through.

Ephraim, the second son of Joseph was born during the seven years of plenty, For Joseph said, "God has caused me to be fruitful in the land of my affliction" (Genesis 41:52). This shows clearly that you can be fruitful even when you are going through some rough seasons, when things look hopeless in man's eyes. God sees and knows the big picture. His grace, His favor, is sufficient to keep you. What an awesome God He is. He is supreme and His name is worthy to be praised.

You, too, may have an appointment with destiny. Do not look at the circumstances. Don't be too logical for without faith it is impossible to please God. You cannot always give your friends a logical reason for your plight, for if they have never done business with God, they would not understand the move you are making.

Scripture says, "And without faith it is impossible to please Him, for he who comes to God must believe that He is, and that He is a rewarder of those who seek him" (Hebrews 11:6 NASB). You want something from God, look to Him and don't tell anybody. He declares Himself to be the Lord. God needs no one. Everything He needs is in Himself. One of His characteristics is in the fact that He is self-existent;

He doesn't need our cake or bread. He is the one who takes nothing and makes something. So, don't look in the wrong direction. God calls individuals who were written off by the public to be employed in His service. Only a privileged few can understand the move of God. Those with an appetite for worship will understand the secret—the mystery; for only a worshipper will share in God's secret.

Those who have been on the mission field over the years, and felt as though the trials were insurmountable, can say today that there is light at the end of the tunnel. We could see a glimmer of light flickering as we move towards the end of the journey. Then and only then we know that we are coming to the finished line. Hallelujah!

Finally, mission is also about community involvement. The church that is involved in missions and pray for missionaries will undoubtedly see tremendous blessings in their ministry. Church growth in this case bound to happen. Many churches don't see missions as an integral part of the ministry, but just a few people who are excited enough to get involved with the neighbor, whether right in their backyard or in a foreign land, will be rewarded openly. I believe totally in this endeavor. It will cause a spiritual awaking in the community and others will become excited, and that excitement will spread like wild fire, causing a new zeal to work for God.

People have been known to sell their property, give away most of their belongings and travel to foreign countries to work on the mission field. Of course, you have to love people enough to want to help them; not just your friends, but people who are not in your locale, people who are different with different background. Of course, church folks are so prejudice and they are the ones who accuse others of being prejudice; but just give them a project and you'll soon find out that they don't really love people. They prefer to sit in church, go in and out and confess Jesus. What have they really done for Him? Absolutely nothing; nonetheless, the door is always open, and this is the right moment to get out there and minister to people. You will experience tremendous blessings as a result of obeying God's Word.

Chapter 20

Destination beyond the norm

As a young woman who has marriage on your list of priorities and probably one of the most exciting moments of your life, you attend a function, and this handsome man comes over and invites you to dance. The party is in full swing, the music has a romantic flare, and he doesn't have two left feet, meaning he is able to move well on the floor. All ends well. Now you must get back to your residence.

You both head for your destination and look forward to meeting again, although you have no idea who this person is or from what kind of material he is made. You might be setting yourself up for rough waters and right now you are not thinking sensibly. You meet again on another occasion and made the decision to be committed, hoping to win the wager that all would be well when you get to know each other. Even now God is not on your list of priorities.

Don't fool yourself

Are you going to consult your parents? Yes, after we get to know each other. Is this how it ought to be? Shouldn't you seek their advice first? What is the procedure? I know according to traditions, in certain cultures, the parents set the stage and make all decisions pertaining to the couple's life in general. And the couples have no problems with that, but even then there can be a climate of deceitfulness within the transaction.

For example, there is a story in the Bible about an arranged marriage that was filled with disappointments, because one parent was not honest in the decision-making arrangements. The story began when Jacob asked his uncle Laban's permission to marry his daughter Rachel. On the wedding night his uncle Laban tricked him, only to find out the next morning that the person lying next to him was Rachel's sister, Leah, whom Jacob did not love. As the first daughter, according to tradition, Leah must marry before Rachel. Jacob was not informed of that procedure before marriage. His uncle handled that very deceitfully, and a series of errors resulted from the arrangement.

Therefore Jacob and his uncle Laban made a contract to work seven years for Rachel. Various problems ensued as a result of this transaction, and Jacob had much more than he bargained for, as his uncle made some unpopular changes in the arrangement causing Jacob to experience some challenges. In trying to defend himself he engaged in some strange dealings in the work force. Much confusion followed that transaction. Therefore, this household is known as "the dysfunctional family."

In the Western world the couple takes responsibility for their lives with no questions asked. They have no one to blame for their decisions but themselves. Although some of their families may show disapproval of the relationship, the couple takes their chances and goes ahead with their plans. Every relationship has a cycle. You fall in love and that's easy. There is no work attached to that. You don't have to exert yourself. We often hear the statement, "I was swept off my feet." You are standing there doing nothing and suddenly something happens to you. As a result, you commit yourself to marriage. After a few years the joy of love grows dim. Slowly but surely, one doesn't pay attention to each other. Your ideas no longer welcome, and all the charm that existed when you first met suddenly disappeared into thin air.

This seems to be the natural course of event with many marriages. However, it's a shame this has to be part of the contract. At this point you ask yourself, would I have done better with my schoolmate whom I left for this character? When you reflect on the euphoria, the question comes to mind, what have I done? How did I get into this mess? Everything seemed so beautiful at the time. What happened? But you are young, innocent, and nothing could go wrong with this relationship. It seemed to be set in heaven. So why is this happening now? Assuming this is part of the territory I didn't hear that expressed in the vow.

After many years of trials it is over. Children are involved, so where do I go from here when my spouse demands that these children stay with him even though I have custody of the four girls. What's more, if I attempt to take them I am constantly threatened with brutality "I will kill them all!" my spouse said. Surely, I am not about to start another war and in the process the children and I are killed. A mother in this predicament requires much wisdom. In fact, she needs God's intervention. She looks at the innocent children, and looks at her spouse—a man capable of doing anything because he is a sick person and lost the power of control. He is recklessly abusive and as a mother I have to employ my safety belt in order to stay alive and have the innocent ones live. Therefore, I must move accordingly, hoping to have peace, even without the children.

What madness! Attempting to manipulate the attorney into letting him have all his wishes even reversing the charge against him, by having the house, no responsibility for alimony, a proposed child support of $45.00 per week for four children and yet he is not satisfied. This is a horrible situation and the beginning of a great spiritual battle. Believe what I'm telling you. It's real! If you have never experienced wickedness, here is witchcraft 101 at its best. The bull is in the arena and I have to face it head on. This is where I need The Almighty God to fight my battle. For the Lord says, "Be not afraid, nor dismayed by reason of this great multitude; for the battle is not yours, but God's" (II Chronicle 20:15). So when the forces of hell come against you, Jesus is the solution. He went through much suffering for us. As a result, He is acquainted with our grief. We have to defend ourselves in the authority of Jesus Christ.

I have known and heard of couples who remarry the same partner and experience even worse situation as in the beginning. And there are those who remarry another partner and suffer the same problem. Few have experienced joy the second time, and I'm happy for them. It would have been foolish of me to become engaged in that same abusive relationship with a sick man who refuses to seek help. That is comparative to committing suicide. Whether or not the curse he pronounced on me had anything to do with it, I remained single and busied myself in higher learning. If you remember, he pronounced that I "will never be happy with another man." The more I became involved with higher education, the better I felt about going on with learning. Despite some setback as a result of the forces of evil, I made it to the end. God is good and His mercy endures forever. Even though it's like hell on earth because I refused to remarry him, anything is better than going back to that abusive jail cell. There are alternatives.

Some individuals have turned to alcohol, some to drugs, others have committed suicide. I busied myself with work, school and ministry. I got involved in missions and made that my priority. When one's spouse refuses to seek counseling, all hope is not lost because God can intervene and do whatever needs to be done, if you will let Him. Of course if we turn away from God the results would be disastrous.

Long distance a plus

In the case where marriages grow fonder during separation by jobs, usually the husband is employed on an airline or working out of state where he would be away for a few days. When they come together it's as though they are beginning a new courtship. According to research, the regular opportunities for separation help most marriages tremendously. After a short separation, both partners are usually longing to see each other. Separation makes the desire to be together a wonderful experience. You often hear the statement, "Distance makes the heart grow fonder." It is a true saying. Many strong happily married women can attest to this. The spouse goes on a business trip and when he returns, love begins to bloom as though they are just beginning a relationship. Sometimes a mini trip together is an asset.

In my case, it was work and more work. When the marriage is laden with obligations such as working daily, at the same time taking care of the children, going on a vacation was never on my priority list. I believe, however, an occasional vacation would put some spark in the marriage. I truly believe that. None of that luxury existed in my marriage. We had to "leave the money in the bank and watch it grow." You remember that? I mentioned it earlier.

I began my marriage with a man who seemed to love me, but who later and even before the marriage showed signs of extreme jealousy, domineering and judgmental manipulation. How-ever, I closed my eyes to that and entered head on into the relationship hoping that change would come. Even during his flirtation with my co-workers and acquaintances, I didn't make it a problem. I pretended not to see, except when I contracted an infection from him during my pregnancy where he, too, had to receive medical treatment. He apologized for that and I was always willing to accept his apologies.

Anger management

Violent marriage ends in divorce. Here comes the possibility of co-parenting. However, those of us who have been in the situation can be fluent about the subject of anger and the possibility of co-parenting after separation. But one has to determine whether or not violence was involved in the marriage. A new study done at the University of Illinois, published in Family Relations revealed some interesting findings. The report revealed the tendency to treat all violence as if it's the same in many cases, but different types of violence requires different interventions, says Jennifer Hardesty, a University of Illinois assistant professor of human and community development.

That makes sense to me. Having tasted the bitterness of abuse, I would never in my wildness imagination believe that all violence is the same, or should be treated as such. Of course they ought to be treated differently in each case.

Also, studies reveal, in some aspects, that the goal is to control the other person and the abuser may use not only physical violence but also psychological and financial abuse to dominate his spouse. This calls for rigid, formal post-divorce safety measures, including supervised visitation of children, and treatment approaches such as a batterer's intervention group or alcoholic or substance treatment. Hardesty's study used in-depth interviews with 25 women to explore differences in their co-parenting relationships with their abusive ex-husbands. Mine was total control of my salary and physical violence to dominate me.

Can you see the dire need for rigid, formal post-divorce safety measures, including supervised visitation of the children? Nonetheless, he took control of that also, and demanded that, even though I have custody of the 4 children—daughters, I dare not have them, as I mentioned earlier. There had not been any heated argument about finances because I gave him full control, and he loved that—just sign the check and place it in his hands. That was fine by me. No problem whatsoever.

Because of my character, he was of the opinion I couldn't leave, for I won't be able to handle any situation without him since he is the one who handled the finances. And so, I worked overtime and, for the first time, cashed my check and bought a personal item for my hair.

Wow! Trouble began in the area of finances. I should never have cashed my check. How dare you cash the check? You have no right, I'm in charge here! The verbal abuse began, and as long as I remained quiet without saying a word, I might escape a beating. So if I'm tempted to speak I know what follows. So, I swallowed my pride and watched for the next move.

New procedure

Because my spouse had become so violent over my cashing that check, I agreed to take the opportunity of handling the household chores, including mortgage payments because he refused to share in the responsibility. Hence I used all my salary to take care of the home, including all bills, without murmuring. Whatever he was trying to prove, I did not give him the opportunity to complain. He kept all his money and I used my salary to take care of the home. He thought I would crumble under the strain, but I remained steadfast with no problem. I was not to have enough sense to handle the business, but I am doing very well, if I may say so myself. Thank God for the opportunity and for His mercy. He is gracious and just and when you think He is not looking at the injustices taking place in your life, I can assure you He is well aware of your situation, but will not give you more than you can bear.

Role differentiation and anger

Studies revealed that role differentiation was a big problem for fathers who had engaged in bitterness and anger. These men had difficulty separating their role as a father from their desire to hold onto their relationship with the mother; and because they were not able to differentiate those roles very well, the mother continued to be the subject of control and abuse even after the separation. In my case, there was no chance of negotiating or even considering this with one who was almost insane in his approach towards me. I was to stay in the abusive situation or the children face death.

According to further study, renegotiating boundaries after divorce poses unique challenges and risks for abused women. Separating from an abusive partner does not necessarily end the violence. In my case, the violence has really just begun with fresh zeal. Separation may threaten an abuser's sense of control and instigate more violence. In such marriages, it may be risky if former partners co-parent after divorce because abusers still have access to their former wives. Women in the study who had been victims of intimate terrorism all continued to be afraid that their ex-husbands would hurt them or their children. That is a perfect scenario of what's happening in my situation. In reality, I can assure you this is exactly what's taking place in an abusive marriage—believe it or not. Those who are afraid to talk about it, and others who insist on staying alive make an effort to take their exit before they die.

These studies are sensitive but very real and true, as I can relate to these women and their testimonies. However, I envy the women who had experienced situational violence in their marriages where co-parenting relationships are carried out with respect for each other. Obviously, there have been no psychological problems in those relationships, and so respecting each other would be the norm. The study shows that currently the legal system assumes it's in a child's best interests to maintain relationships with both parents after divorce. Absolutely, so it should be.

There should be no doubt about that. It's realistic. "As a result, women's attempts to protect their own and their children's safety are often undermined or overlooked." Jennifer said. Obviously, these studies were done without prejudice, mixed with compassion and truth. Any abusive woman in this situation can relate wholeheartedly to this study and the outcome. The average abusive woman can put herself in the center of this research and relate to the truth in that study. In other words, this is no news. It is relative.

Before the divorce, with my spouse's permission, I took the children to Michigan to spend the summer holidays with my sister. Of course I had to get back to work, so I left them in the care of my sisters. I thought a change of atmosphere would be good for them. Unannounced, their father went to Michigan and removed them and brought them back to Brooklyn before the appointed time. It was such a change for them to get out of the abusive situation for the summer, but the duration was curtailed by their father's abrupt intervention, so that he could continue to brainwash them with lies to turn their hearts from me. I felt that talking to them separately would only confuse them. It happens so often where one spouse feeds the children with lies and all kinds of negative stuff, while the other spouse tries to correct the information, leaving the child confused and dejected, not knowing whom to believe. I didn't want this to happen.

Today, when I see how their minds are psychologically ravished, I wish I had told them the truth and have them judge for themselves. Even as adults they are not allowed to think for themselves. But I still believe God is in control and is watching over them.

Emotional abuse

Because it is rather difficult to get the husband to a counselor, and I am speaking from experience, one tries to determine what's the real reason for his refusal to seek help? Does it affect his morale, his ego or his sense of worth? No idea what's in his mind, but his statement is always, "We can work it out together." Yet we never sat down to talk about it, so how are we to work this out? I know for certain that to engage my spouse in such conversation would be like pulling teeth. However, I thought it would be easy to discuss it whenever I mentioned, "Please see a counselor." This statement came up every time he showed his ugly side as he asked for forgiveness. Then it's laid to rest right there. He would not come to terms with the idea that he needed some kind of healing if the marriage were to work. In my spirit I realize he is hiding something. The question regarding his family background would come up, and he would not want to talk about his father. I am just coming to that conclusion.

The wife is more likely to discuss these issues with one in authority. Although in some instances the wife might be so reluctant to talk about it even to a counselor for fear of retaliation by her husband. Because she has to keep everything in her heart and dare not talk about it to anyone, she tends to suffer silently. Also, the more it lingers, it begins to fester and create all kinds of emotional disturbances for both parties.

Many women can attest to that. As a result, therapists tend to go out of their way to engage the man, because he is many times more likely to drop out of counseling sessions than his wife. If the therapist is sufficiently skilled, this extra effort to keep the man engaged isn't a problem in normal relationships. But in sensitive relationships where the wife has to remain silent for fear of brutality, this can turn out to be disastrous because the therapist unwittingly joins with the more resentful, angry, or abusive partner in trying to figure out who is to blame in a given complaint. Most marriage counselors are intelligent and well-meaning and really want to make things better. So they will couch their interventions in terms of what has to be done to resolve the dispute. According to Stephen Stosny, author and therapist in abusive marriages, "women in abusive marriages have to learn to set boundaries. They need to learn skills to make their message work such as making it known that they will not tolerate such behavior any longer." He said, "This is the therapeutic equivalent of a judge dismissing your law suit against vandals because you failed to put up a 'do not vandalize' sign."

I, personally, don't think the average abusive women think about putting up signs, not even in their wildest imagination. It doesn't even cross her mind because she is so taken up with the abusive wounds and the fiery darts that are coming at her. Sometimes depending on the aggressiveness of the abuser, she dare not retaliate or make any such suggestions for fear of getting a double dose. She might want to bring up the statement when things are cool, but even that might flare up into something unpleasant that never would have occurred had she not mentioned what was in her heart. However, I do believe there are many strong, aggressive women out there who might succeed in this approach. In fact, these women are usually not those who are experiencing physical abuse from an almost insane character. They most certainly will not tolerate that nonsense. Consequently, this research group needs to rethink their solution and come up with a feasible, realistic conclusion to fit everyone's situation.

On the contrary, there is another twist by other research workers who revealed that, "putting aside the harmful inaccurate implication that women are abused because they have not the "skill to set boundaries," completely misses the point. Your husband's resentment, anger, or abuse comes from his substitution of power for value. It has nothing to do with the way you set boundaries or with what you argue about. It has to do with his violation of his deepest values. You can be protected, not by setting obvious boundaries that he won't respect, "but by reintegrating your image of yourself that your husband reflects back to you. He will clearly understand that he has to change the way he treats you if he wants to save the marriage."

Again, all this sounds great if you are dealing with a mentally stable individual, in which case, having some confrontation in a marriage relationship may not present a problem. Otherwise you don't want to touch the subject of setting standard in this case. Should the therapist even remotely appear to side with you on any issue, the whole process will be dismissed as some kind of special favor. Some husbands, according to research, blame their wives on the way home from the therapist's office for bringing up threatening or embarrassing things in the counseling session. Couples were known to be seriously injured in car crashes that resulted from arguments on the way home from appointments with therapists. One therapist is certain if you've tried marriage counseling, you've had a few chilly, argumentative, or abusive rides from the session.

Many women live with resentful, angry or abusive men who seem to the rest of the world "charmers." One counselor admits working with cabinet secretaries, billionaires, movie stars, and TV celebrities, all of whom could "charm the fur off a cat, in public." Before they were referred to the counselor, each one of these guys had been championed by marriage counselors who concluded that "their wives were unreasonable, hysterical, or even abusive. They have no trouble at all playing the sensitive, caring husband in therapy. But in the privacy of their homes they sulk, belittle, demean, and even exercise their strong arm."

These men have gotten so good at charming the public, including their marriage counselors, because they've had lots of practice. Since they were young children, they've used charm and social skills to avoid and cover up a monumental collection of core hurts. They are experts at masquerade but there is always someone who is able to detect their schemes. If your husband is a charmer in public, his resentment, anger, or abuse at home is designed to keep you from getting close enough to see how inadequate and unlovable he really feels. In fooling the marriage counselor and the public at large, he makes a fool of you but an even bigger one of himself.

In cases where there was no improvement, the woman refuses to reveal her husband's severe problems with anger and abuse, leaving this wife suffering from acute depression and anxiety that are destroying her physical health. She will not divulge what is really happening in the relationship, and why it is affecting her mentally.

When therapists are aware that their clients are at a very sensitive position at home, they feel almost bound to persuade the woman to leave the relationship. These women are reluctant to reveal the depth of their guilt, shame, and fear of abandonment to their disapproving therapists. Some have reported that their counselors would say things like, "After all he did to you, and you feel guilty?" Therapists have revealed during conferences the amazing position of women whose preferences is to suffer a horrible experience at home rather than moving out of the situation. For example, one report revealed hundreds of therapists at conferences express exasperation about their clients' reluctance to leave their sensitive relationships at home.

Trainings for therapists worldwide always affirm the need of compassion for their clients' heavy burden of guilt. And adding hurt to an already abused woman by making her feel ashamed of her natural feelings of guilt is unacceptable and bad practice. Compassion for her heart-felt hurts is the healthy way to help her deal with her pain.

This gives you an inside view as to what is happening to women throughout the nations. The experiences are horrifying to say the least, having to keep it all inside and not whisper a word to anybody. At least women are able to sit in a counselor's chair for a period of time, where others dare not attend counseling, probably because of fear of retaliation by their abusive partner. Others are threatened by their abusers who insist that they dare not seek counseling or talk to anybody, even to families, about what they are experiencing at home. I, personally, dare not talk to anybody. To be honest, I kept it all from my siblings, so that they would not be accused of giving me advice. Despite all this, my spouse could not believe that my decision to end the marriage was my own doing. Even though I was going through hell, it was impossible for me to make such rash decision on my own. My siblings were not feeling the hurt, I was. There was no reason for them to advise me, especially since I did not share with them the problems I have been going through.

CHAPTER 21

Conflict management

This chapter endeavors to unite the dispute-resolution movement that is impacting society as a whole. Those in the Christian community who deal with conflict on a daily basis through professional practice, ministry, or even attempting to help out a neighbor in distress, will find this invaluable. Also, this can easily apply to conflicts between individuals in homes, churches and the workplace. The information here is based on the premise that knowledge developed in a variety of contexts may be a rich resource for those seeking to help others. Hence the reason I include this chapter. When we refer to the ministry of reconciliation following a conflicting situation, we are describing a ministry all Christians are called to perform, regardless of profession or side interests.

There is an amazing directive from the Word of God, expressed by the apostle Paul in his second letter to the Corinthians, in which he reminds all of us that we are to carry the "message of reconciliation" to the world. Depending on our choice of work as counselors, mediators, ministers, missionaries or leaders in the communities, we may follow the directives along those paths, and in different ways. However, the ministry is the same and I have documented this in chapter eleven. Paul specific words read:

> Therefore, if any man be in Christ, he is a new creature: old things are passed away; behold, all things are become new. And all things are of God, who has reconciled us to himself by Jesus Christ, and has given to us the ministry of reconciliation; To wit, that God was in Christ reconciling the world to himself, not imputing their trespasses unto them; and has committed unto us the word of reconciliation. Now then we are ambassadors for Christ, as though God did beseech you by us: we pray you in God's stead, be ye reconciled to God.
>
> —2 Corinthians 5:17-20

For example, Paul's letter to the Corinthian church expressed his disappointment in a church he invested considerable time, a church he had founded and visited to see its' progress. His letter reveals that this church was not what he had envisioned when he started it. He expressed concerns about the lack of Christian values and relationships, divisions in the church, conflict as to whom the Corinthian Christians should be following, sexual immorality, lawsuits among believers, conflict in marriage and over divorce, the worshiping of idols, and lack of love for each other. Take note of this, Paul was also concerned about the conflicts between those who believed Christians have liberty in the Lord, and those who wanted to bind their fellow Christians to tradition or specific practices. Many of us can relate to this portion. The Corinthians were at odds about how people came together to participate in the Lord's Supper, and the role of women in worship. Their conflict also related to spiritual gifts, and the lack of unity among believers. The apostle was writing to a church that really was in trouble—a church that had enough conflict to keep counselors and ministers busy for years. He did not hesitate to express his disappointment. His second letter to the believers in Corinth expressed his joy and confidence in the believers, and reminded them that they had been reconciled and were still being reconciled, and that they were to continue to engage in the ministry of reconciliation. The apostle's primary concern was reconciliation between all people and God. He was also concerned about human relationships with each other. In addition, the Corinthians' conflict over all the other things listed was of great concern to Paul. Therefore, he sought to encourage their reconciliation and unity. We, too, can help others move toward reconciliation by sharing our own experiences.

So, the apostle Paul is a good example of what reconciliation can do for you personally. Known as Saul at the time, Paul persecuted the Christians in a radical way. Yet after his personal reconciliation with the Lord Jesus, he was totally changed from persecutor to a minister of the Word of God. Looking back on the change in his own life, Paul knew that if God could bring about a change in him, God could do the same for you and me. It is important to have a vision or a testimony of how God takes you from one bad situation, and manifests Himself in your life, to fulfill His plan in you and your family.

Having a testimony can be a tremendous blessing for others in your ministry. I should have been dead but God spared my life to testify of His awesomeness. He can do the same for you. Many people are hurting and in the midst of conflict, and are looking for encouragement. Even though their behavior was constantly at odds, the Corinthians always had an encouraging word from Paul who had a vision about how they could be reconciled to God, and to each other. Even in the midst of harsh conflict we can predict harmony.

Working in the medical field that was unionized for non-professionals, I always heard the word "bargaining table" in a conflicting situation. Conflict was at its highest among union non-professionals. It was a noisy atmosphere even in the hallway, at the dining table, in the parking lot. Getting to the bargaining table when both parties are certain "I am right" on one side of the table, and "I am right" on the other side of the table, takes courage beyond measure. One has to be really skilled in dealing with reconciliation. Most of the times, God is not at the center at the bargaining table, so the argument is always boisterous vocally.

In defense of his ministry, the apostle Paul writes, "For though we walk in the flesh, we do not war after the flesh: For the weapons of our warfare are not carnal, but mighty through God to the pulling down of strong holds;" (2 Corinthians 10:4). This means, it's a spiritual battle. Neglecting the Word spells disaster. We must apply the Word of God if we are to be victorious. Otherwise, the individuals will not be affected by the ministry of reconciliation. In other words, sitting at the bargaining table where the atmosphere is boisterous, you must invite the Lord Jesus to give you peace. He says, "Peace I leave with you, my peace I give unto you: not as the world gives . . . Let not your heart be troubled, neither let it be afraid" (John 14:27).

How does this affect me?

After I had worn out of options, my final decision was to get out of the abusive situation with what was made available to me. Much later, included in my doctoral studies in theology was a study in Counseling and Conflict management which I found most valuable in dealing with the Christian community. However, I wonder if this would have been beneficial to me in an abusive relationship, especially when the abuser bluntly refused counseling. Conflict management might even prove to be offensive, and might require a strong arm to help in the referee encounter across the table with no accomplishments, when all is said and done.

You are likely to see the real person when the man is asked to come to terms with his anger in the presence of the bargaining committee. Instead of waiting until he gets home and lashing out behind closed doors, he might have to demonstrate his real character at the bargaining table. I say this because the abusive spouse hides that aspect of his character in the presence of outsiders. His is charming, cool, calm and collective to the public. We cannot expect him to expose his real self by letting out steam in public. The individuals see him as Don Won—handsome and charming, now witnessing a completely different character. Shakespeare once said, you can fool some of the people some of the time, but you cannot fool all of the people all of the time. The elements will catch up with you eventually. This is the reason my spouse couldn't fool the judge on that final day in court 20 years after the divorce. After that final decision he was so crushed, even more violent, that he went home and gave the children a double dose of his therapeutic medicine for mind control.

Today, the world is so well-informed that the average person is not able to fool it. Even my last session in court lets me know that the judge was not ready to be taken for a ride by some smart dude, or one who thinks he can outsmart everybody. He was not just educated and smart, his character depicted a man of sensitivity, one who was not operating in the valley realm, but obviously was in touch with a higher authority. He could see through my spouse's controlling spirit and refused to bargain with him and his tricks. Thank God for giving wisdom to judges in the courtroom to be able to make wise decisions, and to recognize those folks who set out to hoodwink them and their surroundings.

My spouse had no trouble at all playing the sensitive, caring husband when he insisted on taking the children to court just to watch him charm those in his presence. Those children were made to forego their education to begin a brainwash therapy by their father. This masquerade happened more than once. I am so happy to know that this did not affect their final grades. Even now he wouldn't let go, but I thank God who has kept me from death. Even as I am still faced with the evil, the Lord is constantly feeding me with songs and a Word from the Bible. He is faithful and expects me to trust Him despite the situation.

God lets me know that he is at my side

Here is a Bible verse that the Lord reiterated to my attention: "Trust in the Lord with all your heart and lean not unto your own understanding. In all your ways acknowledge him and he will direct your path" (Proverbs 3: 5-6)

The Lord has convinced me that in order to survive the trials of life, it is imperative that I trust Him. So, when you are going through pressures of life open your Bible to Proverbs Chapter Three and read the precious Word of God. As I meditate on these words it reminds me that I need to use my situation as an opportunity to exercise faith, to believe that the Lord will see me through regardless of how impossible it looks.

There are many other Scriptures that will encourage you. In fact, the Bible is replete with answers for every situation in our lives. This is the manner in which the Lord communicates with me. I must live by faith. The Scripture says, "Faith is the substance of things hoped for and the evidence of things not seen" (Hebrews 11:1). To explain faith more explicitly, putting it this way, Faith is: "believing God with all your heart, despite your circumstances."

Therefore, you can accomplish your goal and your dreams if you act on God's Word by faith. I am not saying it is easy, especially when the mountain in front of you does not make room for you to move. But the Lord said all we need to do is speak to the mountain, and if you have faith it will crumble before your eyes. To do that we must have confidence in the one who is the Author and Finisher of our faith, Jesus Christ, our Lord.

You have to keep on hoping because there's much in store for you in the kingdom of God. Faith prepares you for what lies ahead. Again, the Bible is replete with solutions for your decision. All you need to do is search the Scriptures daily for the golden nuggets that are in the pages before your eyes. If you are seeking to be healed, the answer is in the Bible. If you are seeking deliverance, there is an answer in the Scriptures. It is there you will find wisdom.

Again, the Scripture says, "For God has not given us the spirit of fear, but of power, and of love, and of a sound mind" (2 Timothy 1:7). The adversary would love to get you in a corner and instill fear. But you are to keep your mind on heavenly things. The Scripture speaks of keeping your mind on things above. Focus on the Lord, stay in the Word and know that God will see you through your valley experience. He will bring you out if you put faith to work. This means, while the victory is not yet visible to the naked eye, you can see it in the spirit. You must believe, regardless of how it looks. You are to be spiritually minded and expect a miracle. In fact, you can see the victory in your mind's eye.

The Lord will challenge you to see where your thoughts are, because He knows you cannot function without Him. He does this to grow your faith as you learn to rely on Him to take care of your problems. Many times the Lord will give you a biblical solution straight from the Bible. He is an awesome God. We are commanded to meditate on the Word of God. For example, the book of Joshua Chapter One is full of encouraging word. It lets us know that we must be strong and courageous, and must stay focus on the Word. "Turn not from it to the right hand or to the left that you may prosper wherever you go" (Joshua 1: 7).

The whole summary of this chapter is found in verse 8, "This book of the law shall not depart out of your mouth; but you shall meditate therein day and night, that you may observe to do according to all that is written therein: for then you shall make your way prosperous, and then you shall have good success" (Joshua 1:8).

I feel such compassion for those who don't know the value of searching the Scriptures, for in it there is much information to comfort you in every situation. I was there at one time, a time when I wished I knew the Bible, even to get a glimpse of it. But I knew enough to lift my hands to heaven and cry out, "Lord, please help me!" Later when I began to delve into the Scriptures and found that Peter did not need a multitude of words, when he began to sink while walking on the water to meet Jesus. You see, Peter had taken his eyes off Jesus for a moment, and beginning to sink he cried out, "Lord save me!" And immediately Jesus stretched forth his hand, and caught him, and said unto him, "O you of little faith, why did you doubt?" (Matthew 14: 22-31).

The apostle Paul shares his stressful moments through his epistles. One example in particular is found in the book of Second Corinthians. It reads: "We are troubled on every side yet not distressed; we are perplexed, but not in despair; persecuted, but not forsaken, cast down, but not destroyed; always bearing about in the body the dying of the Lord Jesus that the light also of Jesus might be made manifest in our body" (2 Corinthians 4:8-10).

These are the words that will cause you to ponder when you realize what you have been going through, believing you will come forth like gold tried in the fire. Can you imagine gold having a makeover? When God is ready to re-shape you, He becomes the goldsmith who melts you and molds you and shapes you in a way pleasing to Him. You can think of Daniel in the den of lions; you can think of the three Hebrew boys thrown in the fiery furnace and God delivered them with no hurt; not even a singe on their clothing. Instead, a fourth man was seen walking around the fiery furnace. It was the Lord presenting Himself as He came to their rescue. What an awesome miracle. God is still in the miracle business today if only we can trust Him for what He says in His Word. His promises are true.

Therefore, trying to fight with the servants of God is coming against God Himself. The prophet Daniel was a faithful servant of God living in an idolatrous environment with no fault of his own. His faithfulness to God got him in trouble with the king. Because Daniel refused to partake of the king's meat and prayed openly three times daily, he was thrown into the den of lions. The Scripture tells us, "The king gave the order, and they brought Daniel and threw him into the lions' den." The king said to Daniel, "May your God, whom you serve continually, rescue you!" They placed a stone over the mouth of the den, and the king sealed it with his own signet ring, so that Daniel's situation might not be changed. Then the king returned to his palace and spent the night without eating and without having any entertainment and he could not sleep. Despite the decree, the king was concerned about Daniel.

After fasting during the night, the king got up and hurried to the lion's den and called to Daniel in an anguished voice. "Daniel, servant of the living God, has your God, whom you serve continually, been able to rescue you from the lions?" Daniel answered, "O king, live forever! My God sent his angel to shut the mouths of the lions. They have not hurt me, because I was found innocent in his sight. Nor have I ever done any wrong before you, O king." The king was overjoyed and gave orders to lift Daniel out of the den with no wound, no hurt, because he had trusted in his God. At the king's command Daniel's accusers were brought in and thrown into the den of lions along with their wives and children. Before they reached the floor of the den, the lions overpowered them and crushed all their bones. (Daniel 6:16-24). What an awesome God we serve. We simply ought to remain faithful to Him despite the enemy's bombardment.

Daniel, a man greatly beloved of God, refused to partake of the king's meat and continued to pray three times a day. Because of jealousy, the administrators set out to trap Daniel. To do so they encouraged the king to make a decree, demanding worship to his god. However, Daniel refused to worship the king's gods. As his custom, he insisted on worshipping Almighty God openly. That infuriated the administrators. But Daniel's faithfulness is a good example for every believer. Remain faithful no matter what comes against you, and God will take care of your enemy. Likewise his three friends, Shadrach, Meshach, and Abednego were cast into the burning fiery furnace for the same reason. They were worshippers. For this reason they were placed in a fiery furnace, but God delivered them unharmed.

At times I can hear God whisper into my spirit, "Take your eyes off your circumstances and get creative in me." Push yourself and get involved in the affairs of God, then, after you have accomplished your goal, even talking to the core sinner and watch him come to Christ because of the strategy God placed in you. Then testify in the church about the wonderful things Jesus has accomplished in your life. God will give you the courage to go through the fire. After the Lord brings you out, you might say, it was good training. The effect on me was well worth it.

The apostle Paul writes about his reaction to his suffering in the book of Corinthians. He takes pleasure in suffering. When you get a biblical perspective about this you begin to stop focusing on limitations such as the persecutions, the pain and trouble that accompany those trials. Apostle Paul writes, "When I am weak then I am strong." To change your whole perspective on life, God is setting you up for something bigger than you are. It starts with weakness—humility.

Look at that picture strung out on the cross—His weakness became the most powerful transformation. It's all started in weakness. But death, burial and the resurrection is a work of the Almighty God. Take a spiritual view of this. You may be experiencing problems or worrying about trouble in the world. If you base your faith on the news, you easily can conclude that there is no peace on earth. But God sent Jesus to bring you a different kind of peace, a peace that passes all understanding. He gives you victory over the power of the enemy. Today, remember that God is alive. He has a great plan for your life. Because of His love, he left His Divinity, took on humanity and manifested Himself through a virgin birth so that we might have eternal life. Rest in Him. The Scripture reads, "Rest in the Lord and wait patiently for him: Fret not yourself because of him who prospers in his way, because of the man who brings wicked devices to pass" (Psalm 37:7). It's resting in Jesus Christ, surrendering completely to Him. Resting in Him means free of worry and murmuring.

To reiterate, often the Lord gives me a Word straight from the Bible, just to let me know that despite what I'm going through He is there. Recently, He had a sister call me at 6 a.m. to sing this song to me. I had never heard it sung before, but the word comes from Psalm 124: "If it had not been the LORD who was on our side when men rose up against us: (Psalm 124:1). She sang these words, "If it had not been the LORD who was on my side where would I be." What an awesome God we serve. He never ceases to amaze me. He often gives me a word, also encourages me through his messengers. I am encouraged by the Word from this Scripture: "Worry about nothing; but in everything by prayer and supplication with thanksgiving let your requests be made known unto God. And the peace of God, which passes all understanding, shall keep your hearts and minds through Christ Jesus" (Philippians 4:6-7). And because the enemy uses a spirit of deception to try and control your mind, the following verse is particularly useful. It reads, "Finally, brethren, whatsoever things are true, whatsoever things are honest, whatsoever things are just, whatsoever things are pure, whatsoever things are lovely, whatsoever things are of good report; if there be any virtue, and if there be any praise, think on these things. Those things which you have both learned, and received, and heard, and seen in me, do: and the God of peace shall be with you"

—Philippians 4:8-9

God always has something for you. After it is made clear in your spirit, grab hold of it and never let it go. The enemy would like to have you focus on your circumstances instead of what God has in store for you. Stay with the vision and fight the enemy with every fiber of your being through the Word of God. You are going to need strength from God to accomplish the task. Be defiant and remain determined to hold on to God's Word. Let me tell you, you are going to need every ounce of strength you can muster and it comes only from God.

Even ministers and pastors are throwing in the towel today; but my advice to you is hold on tight, the enemy is not stronger than God. This is why knowing the Word at an early age is so vital. Mine was at a ripe age, even though I grew up in the church and never missed a Sunday. As far as introduction to the Bible, that was nowhere in my territory. In fact, I did not possess a Bible. The mass book was all there was in the home.

Nonetheless, when I came to the understanding, in addition to someone introducing me to the Bible, I refused to lay it down. The rich Word in these 66 books is a treasure not to be neglected. Sometimes, just when you have a special plan to accomplish, God will have you change your agenda. Still, don't question Him. He knows what He is doing and where He is taking you. Trust Him to take you there. It might be painful on the way, in fact, very painful. However, hold on to that pathway, because there is victory at the end of the race.

After I had gone through my divorce it was clear to me that I had a purpose in life. I was not quite sure what that purpose was, but I kept getting visions that were not clear. A new convert, not having the proper guidance, I didn't take them seriously. Much later when I received the full understanding of my calling, it was clear that my mission was ordained by God.

God is seeking for those who would carry out the dream He has placed in your hearts. Don't expect positive feedback from those around you. They will discourage you by trying to show you how risky this mission is. "Are you sure you heard from God?" some would ask. Or, "It is too dangerous out there to minister on the streets of New York."

I agree, it is dangerous, but if God calls you He will protect you. It is dangerous to disobey the call of God. Whenever you are to move out on a journey for the kingdom you have to take risks. Even the church folks would discourage you because they are not going anywhere themselves. They will hinder your progress every time, and look at you as being odd; and their negativity will keep you from obtaining God's promise for your life. Know that if no one criticizes you in or out of the church, it's a sure sign you are not doing anything worthwhile for God. The key is, don't let anyone intimidate you and cause you to miss the plan of God for your life. Stay close to Jesus and become engulfed with the fire that is within you. He has placed greatness within you. Once you recognize that, the ball is in your court. It is up to you to grab hold and run with it, in the name of Jesus. I found this out much later in life, and I love it.

CHAPTER 22

Prayer changes things

Do you ever feel that your prayers don't make a difference? That God doesn't hear you when you pray? Do you wonder if praying is a waste of time? If these thoughts bombard you, listen to what the Bible says about prayer. The apostle John had a vision which he explained in the book of revelation. He saw a Lamb who "came and took the book out of the right hand of the One who sat on the throne." Before the throne were 24 elders who "fell down before the Lamb." Each of them was holding "golden bowls full of incense, which are the prayers of the saints" (Revelation 5:7-8). In this we see a picture of all of our prayers being collected before the throne of God. We see prayers of all kinds—long prayers, short prayers, prayers from children and adults, prayers from new believers and experienced spiritual warriors. Your prayers are included in this collection. Every time you pray, picture your prayers as part of that collection before God's throne. None of your prayers are forgotten, and all of them make a difference. Just as God holds you in high regard as His child, so does your prayers. You and your prayers are valuable, and God looks forward to having a dialogue with you on a daily basis.

Are there people you know who have needs? Do you have problems that need to be addressed? Do you need wisdom and direction in your life? Do you have a burden to pray for your nation or for the problems in the world? You might have been praying about a matter for months or years, but God wants you to continue to be bold in petitioning Him with these needs. Don't be discouraged or give up hope. The Bible is replete with solutions. Apart from many other examples, whenever I need an encouraging word from the Lord, I like to open my Bible to Joshua Chapter One and it reads:

"No man shall be able to stand before you all the days of your life. As I was with Moses, so I will be with you; I will not fail you or forsake you. Be strong (confident) and of good courage, for you shall cause this people to inherit the land which I swore to their fathers to give them. Only you be strong and very courageous . . ." (Joshua 1:5-7 Amplified).

Always remember, from the moment you set your heart to pray, God hears you and your prayers are being received before His throne. He says, "Let us therefore come boldly unto the throne of grace, that we may obtain mercy, and find grace to help in time of need" (Hebrews 4:16). Yes, we are privileged to seek God with boldness. We don't need a third party, go directly to God and join the elders in heaven by spending time worshipping Him.

In the book of Revelation Chapters four, five, seven, and eleven are perfect examples of worship. Then make some noise as you read Chapter Nineteen. The 24 elders bowed down and worshipped God, committing everything to Him. Make prayer your priority in the midst of your trials.

Taking my own time with this writing, I am relaxing this morning, in no hurry to get out of bed. Suddenly, the Lord instilled in my heart the need to get this writing completed soon. I rose from my slumber, got myself together, on the computer and tried to put the puzzles together. It was as though The Lord was saying, "hurry up with this project because I have something else for you in the making. He has already asked me to get back to the music, but I have very little time to sit at the piano. The awesomeness of God, my Father, is indescribable. He makes sure I am aware of His presence in what I do and what He ordains for me. The author of the book of Hebrews left an encouraging word to the young converts who were being persecuted for the Gospel, and were tempted to return to Judaism. He wrote: "Let us run with patience the race that is set before us, looking unto Jesus, the author and finisher of our faith . . ." (Hebrews 12: 1-2)

In other words, things might look as though you are not progressing and everything seems to be lying dormant, nonetheless victory is around the corner. Don't give up! It doesn't matter how many obstacles the adversary throws at you, hold on to this Scripture: "No weapon that is formed against you shall prosper; and every tongue that shall rise against you in judgment you shall condemn. This is the heritage of the servants of the Lord, and their righteousness is of me, says the Lord" (Isaiah 54:17). God always has an encouraging word for His children as long as we don't set Him aside and treat Him as second best.

Always know how to have a dialogue with God in your sleeping and in your waking; in your travel, as you move around the house, in your shopping, and on the job. The battle is God's but you have to involve yourself in Him. Enfold yourself in Him, and He will see you through. Prayer is the key and prayer changes things. However, the Bible tells us about effective prayer as opposed to prayer that might not reach heaven, depending on how ineffective they are.

An example of effective prayer

In First Chronicles Chapter Four, there is a wonderful example of prayer. It is about a young man who built his hope on the Lord, and heaven took notice of his prayer and supplication. He needed to change his circumstances in order to live comfortably in his society. Therefore, he decided to have a conversation with God. In fact, he prayed earnestly and asked God to shoot him out of his present situation.

He looked at himself and his circumstances and saw no reason to move on in life unless there was a change in his surroundings. That required a name change. He prayed the boldest, most hopeful prayer you could imagine and God answered him. Jabez means "son of pain," a descendant of Judah, but from what family we don't know. The only mention made of him is in this remarkable account: "And Jabez was more honorable than his brothers; but his mother named him Jabez, saying, 'Because I bore him in pain'" (1Chronicles 4:9).

The Scripture says Jabez called on the God of Israel saying, "O, that you would bless me indeed, and enlarge my territory, that your hand would be with me, and that you would keep me from evil that I may not cause pain." So God granted him that which he requested" (1 Chronicle 4:9-10). He will cause pain." This is the literal meaning of the name his mother gave him when he was born. The Bible says she gave him the name because she "bore him in pain."

However, it was Jabez who had to carry the burden of the name throughout his life. He didn't sit and mourn and complain about it, but was smart enough to know that there is a God, a Father who could do something about this predicament, so he prayed earnestly to the God who answers prayer. First, he asked God to bless him. Lord, you are the giver of all good things. I need you to overshadow me with every blessing you can give to me. Be gracious to me, you are a good God and everything I need is in your storehouse. Even though I am not worthy, you are a merciful God. Bless me, Lord, and I will not forget to worship you, in Jesus' name.

Secondly, according to the Scripture, Jabez pleaded for more territory with more influence and more responsibility. Lord, thank you for making me in your own image, and for securing an important destiny for me. I want to fulfill your dream for me all the days of my life, in the precious name of Jesus.

Finally, Jabez asked for power. Oh "that your hand would be with me, and that you would keep me from evil." Lord, reach down from heaven and put your mighty hand on me. I desire your strength working in me, through me and around me, to do your work. Please empty me of self and fill me with the fullness of your Spirit to experience joy unspeakable and your glory beyond measure, in the name of Jesus Christ.

Great importance acquired from this request, is sufficient to make it worthy of being handed down only from God's having so fulfilled his wish. His life became a contradiction of his name, the son of pain having been free from pain in life, and having attained to greater happiness and reputation than his brothers. This simple prayer is a wonderful truth that God blesses those who faithfully call upon Him.

Note that Jabez was "more honorable than his brothers" (v. 9). His life and prayer demonstrated how God delights to bless those who call upon Him in faith and earnestly seek His favor. When you think of the God who is more than enough, a cattle on a thousand hills belongs to Him. He says, "Ask, and it shall be given you; seek and you shall find; knock, and it shall be opened unto you" (Matthew 7:7). Sometimes we neglect to take God seriously. Every word that He promises is true and He will fulfill it as long as it is in His will.

He is the same God today. You, too, can cry out to God to shoot you out of your present situation. You can reach out to Him for the great plans He has for you. The same thing God did for Jabez He can do for you, also. He has a purpose for your life. Seek Him daily. He is such a great Father, always ready to listen to His children. All you have to do is get close to Him. How do you do that? Read His Word day and night. This is one method of having fellowship with Him. Simply invite Him into your house, sit quietly and have a talk with Him as you read the Word during your devotion. You will be surprised how that closeness will develop into a beautiful relationship. He is a good listener. He loves you more than you ever know. Please take a chance on Him. He is an awesome God.

Jabez could have accepted this pain as fate. He could have been resentful, bitter, or angry. Instead, he went to God and asked Him to change his circumstance. He insisted he was not about to remain in that position and asked God to shoot him out of it. Even though his name tended to hinder his progress, the Scripture says he was more honorable than the rest of the family. Despite the fact that he was more honorable, his name didn't carry that nobility. So, he had to do something about it. The good news is that God granted his requests. The Bible reminds us that our God can change any circumstance. No problem is too big for Him. You may feel trapped in hopelessness. You may be haunted by mistakes you have made, or by the words of others. You may have financial needs, physical disabilities, or a limited education. But the story of Jabez shows us that God can shoot you out of that jail cell and renew your mind. The book of Romans tells us, "Be not conformed to this world: but be transformed by the renewing of your mind, that you may prove what is that good, and acceptable, and perfect, will of God" (Romans 12:2).

Today, remember that God can change your circumstances. He will give you a new start in life. He wants you to be bold. Confess His Word. Believe Him for favor and victory. The Scripture says, "Weeping may endure for a night, but joy comes in the morning" (Psalm 30:5).

If I were sitting around feeling sorry for myself I would not be standing here to share this information with you. On the contrary, God is available 24 hours a day. His telephone line is never engaged. You will not get a busy signal. He invites you to come boldly to His throne room and ask, believing that He will answer whatever your needs are. Today are you feeling hopeless? Are you feeling discouraged? Are you worried or afraid? You have the opportunity to experience new joy today. Stand on God's Word. Praise Him. Worship Him. Trust Him.

Jabez began his life with a handicap, and his mother named him Jabez "because I bore him in pain." Yet Jabez didn't let a hurtful past or an unpromising present keep him from asking God for a huge blessing. Did you begin your life with a disadvantage? Here is an example. Are you facing shame or rejection? Do you feel like a useless person? Negative life experiences can profoundly influence how you see yourself and how you understand and relate to God. They can change the way you pray, cutting you off from God's abundant best. You can survive these difficult times by having faith in God. You can have confidence that He will bring you to safety. I can attest to that. His mercy is without measure.

Are you going through storms in your life? Do you feel battered and shaken, like you'll never find peace? In times like these remember to stand on the promises of God. He is trustworthy. Look to Him in every situation you face. He will bring you through safely, to a new day. Remember you are special in God's sight. Consider the unique gifts and talents He's given you. You must realize how important it is to use these gifts and talents. Do what He has called you to do. Seek to be fruitful and productive for the Kingdom of God. Nothing can prevent the Word of God from being fulfilled. Know that you can confide in Him and be confident in His sovereignty, confident in His eternal design, confident that He can and will shape everything to accomplish His purposes in your life. Be confident He is with you in every battle and will give you victory. Recognize that Jesus Christ is the key to everything in your life, your success, your peace, and your security. Trust in Him; He is the one who shed His blood on the cross for you.

Today, commit your decisions to God. Seek to become more sensitive to the signs and signposts He provides for you. Wait for Him, even when your mind and emotions may urge you to move. Be willing to walk by faith, not by sight. Fill your mind with His Word, and let it shape your thoughts. Commit yourself to walking in the light, for He is the light of the world.

Hindrance by the forces of evil

The book of Revelation describes Satan's forces as spirits armed with power, even "performing signs." Their goal is to fight against God's people, to gather the nations against God, and to accomplish Satan's purposes. But the Bible tells us that Jesus came to the earth "to destroy the works of the devil" (1John 3:8). He frequently cast out demons and gave His disciples "power and authority over all the demons" (Luke 9:1). Yet we are warned that Satan can be subtle, for he's "a liar and the father of lies" (John 8:44). He can appear in any form, even as an angel of light" (2 Corinthians 11:14).

Although Satan may try to frighten you through dreams or by filling your mind with negative thoughts, through the blood of Jesus you have the victory. You must use the power and authority God has given you. Don't allow Satan to gain an advantage over you. Don't be ignorant of his schemes" (2 Corinthians 2:11). You must take this spiritual battle seriously. This is not a movie, but real life, with eternal consequences. Put on your spiritual armor. Be strong in the Lord. Be filled with God's Word and faith instead of fear, and declare victory in the name of Jesus.

God always has something for you. When it is made clear in your spirit, grab hold and run with it. Always remember, the enemy would like to have you focus on your circumstances instead of on God, so that you cannot get a clear understanding of the vision. So, my advice to you is, stay close to Jesus and fight with every fiber of your being. The Scripture says the battle is God's. Therefore, in your attempt to fight, please know that God is right there to fight for you. Be defiant. Be determined to hold on to Jesus. Let me tell you, you are going to need every ounce of strength which comes only from God. Rest in Him. Don't throw in the towel. The pastors who are giving up, need to know that the enemy is not stronger than God. Have praying people around you for daily intercessory prayer.

This is why knowing the Word of God at an early age is so vital. When I got hold of the Word I held on to it by making it my daily devotion. No one was able to hinder me from reading the Scriptures. Sometimes you might have the urge to do great things for God, but feel incapable because of those around you, or because of the name that was given to you at birth, like Jabez, or someone in particular causing trouble. For this reason, you must do something about the situation, for you know without a doubt, you have a real purpose in life. Likewise, I do believe God is seeking for those who would carry out the dream he has placed in your hearts. Take the chance and move out on God's call for your life. Stay away from your negative associates. They will keep you from obtaining God's promises. Don't let fear paralyze you, and don't be put off by people's speech and miss the fulfillment of the dream God has placed in you. Stay close to Jesus and become engulfed in the fire that will set you ablaze to do the work. Then you can say like the prophet Jeremiah, "The word was in my heart as a burning fire shut up in my bones" (Jeremiah 20:9). Yes, this is the effect of the Word when you get hold of it.

No matter how hard the prophet Jeremiah tried, he was unable to suppress God's message within him. He sympathized fully with God's anger against the sins of the people. The prophet felt such oneness with God and His cause that he had to proclaim the Word of the Lord, even though that mission brought excruciating pain and suffering.

There are many examples in the Bible of people who were trying to block the progress of God's work. In the book of Numbers Chapters Twenty-two-Twenty-Five, the Medianites were determined to stop God's people. As a result, they joined with the Moabites to hire Balaam to curse the Israelites. This plot failed, but soon some of the Israelites yielded to temptation and engaged themselves in idolatry with the Medianites. Determined to keep the Israelite's community pure, God commanded that all who had given themselves to false gods were to be eliminated. As they dealt with this crisis, an Israeli man brought a Medianite woman into the community. This was a horrible violation of God's laws. Aaron's son, Phinehas, earned special praise by piercing this man and woman with a spear. (Numbers 25: 16-18)

Concerned about keeping His people pure, God was angry with the Medianites because they had deceived His people by trickery. God hated this conduct. He detests a person of deceit. He says those who practice "deceit shall not dwell within my house" (Psalm 5:6). Likewise those who speak falsely "shall not maintain his position before me" (Psalm 101:7). Lies and deceit originated in the Garden of Eden when Satan deceived Eve. To reiterate, Jesus tells us that Satan is the "father of lies," and "there is no truth in him" (John 8:44). Those who lie and deceive are simply following Satan's examples and influences.

Many individuals are influenced by his deception. Even believers can be guilty of lies and deceit. Instead of being people of integrity, totally committed to God, they can resort to trickery in their business dealings, in interpersonal relationships, in families, marriages, and even with church families. If you want to please God, seek to eliminate deceit from your life. Don't submit to Satan's tricks and temptation. Instead, cultivate a life of purity. Speak the truth. Be an honest ambassador of God's Kingdom in everything you do. As we take stock of ourselves we can look back at Israel's position. It was a time for a new census. Nearly 40 years had passed since the Israelites' first census took place soon after they had left Egypt. Much had happened in the intervening years. The adults from that earlier generation had died, and a new generation had arisen. There were new leaders, and they were beginning a new era in their history. They were in a new place and about to face a whole new series of circumstances—new enemies and adversaries, new challenges and problems; and they were about to enter the Promised Land. It was time for this new generation to be counted—time to take a new look at God's people, take stock of who would take a stand, and determine what roles everyone would play and how they would proceed.

As the Israelites faced their new day, each of us must realize that God is the God of new beginnings, of second chances, and of opportunities to start over again. You can learn from the past, but you always must move forward. As you repent and learn from your mistakes, you must never allow them to cripple you or dominate your life. When you think of your past, you must remember that God's "compassion never fails. They are new every morning" (Lamentations 3:22-23).

Today, you have the opportunity to live in the past, to think about opportunities lost, mistakes made, things you have done or should have done. But although God wants you to learn from the past, He also calls you to commit the past to Him. Confess your sins, and accept His forgiveness. Declare that this is a new day for you. Face your future filled with freedom, boldness, and confidence in Him knowing that every upset is a learning process. You learn to depend on Him as you go through the valley with no apparent outlet. But just wait, you will get to the mountaintop if you persevere and hold on with patience.

Reflecting on the words "hold on," this poem comes to mind:

> If you can keep your head when all about you
> Are losing theirs and blaming it on you,
> If you can trust yourself when all men doubt you
> But make allowance for their doubting too.
> If you can wait and not be tired of waiting,
> Or being lied about, don't deal in lies,
> Or being hated don't give way to hating,
> And yet don't look too good or talk too wise.

If you can dream and not make dreams your master,
If you can think and not make thoughts your aim,
If you can meet with Triumph and Disaster
And treat those two imposters just the same;
If you can bear to hear the truth you've spoken
Twisted by knaves to make a trap for fools,
Or watch the things you gave your life to, broken,
And stoop and build them up with worn-out tools:

If you can make one heap of all your winnings
And risk it on one turn of pitch-and-toss,
And lose, and start again at your beginnings
And never breathe a word about your loss;
If you can force your heart and nerve and sinew
To serve your turn long after they are gone,
And so hold on when there is nothing in you
Except the Will which says to them: 'Hold on!'

If you can talk with crowds and keep your virtue,
Or walk with kings or lose the common touch,
If neither foes nor loving friends can hurt you,
If all men count with you, but none too much;
If you can fill the unforgiving minute
With sixty seconds' worth of distance run,
Yours is the Earth and everything that's in it
And which is more—you'll be a man, my son.

By

Rudyard Kipling

If you meditate on the words of this poem it will minister to you as you encounter trials, wrong accusation and all manner of evil. It will encourage you to hold on despite the injustices. The Lord Jesus says in the Gospel of John, "These things I have spoken unto you, that in me you might have peace. In the world you shall have tribulation, but be of good cheer; I have overcome the world" (John 16:33). It is important to quote the written word over your life in distress, in sickness, and in every condition you are experiencing in your life.

The Bible is replete with information that will keep Satan at bay. This does not mean that he is going to give up the first time. He will try to hinder you in every way he can, as he is doing with the pastors who are giving up. He will try to keep your ministry from moving on. So we ought to know how to take authority over the situation in our marriages and our ministry.

Fear for your life can be all the motivation you need to stay in an abusive relationship. However, even though throughout my life my spouse continued to threaten my life with the use of indulging in evil after the separation, I might have been dead had I stayed in the relationship. Others stay in an abusive relationship because of insecurity, believing that they would not be able to handle themselves apart from the marriage. A good education is invaluable; something you can depend on for your future. It is also important to have a profession.

One person admits that her husband first convinced her to go to counseling because he thought the counselor would tell her that she needed to change. But when he didn't hear what he wanted, he quitted and forbade her to ever go again. In my case I had to leave before the violence escalated into a potentially life-threatening situation. In fact, it was always a life-threatening situation. Your life could be in grave danger when you are dealing with insanity.

After my encounter in the prison, I was determined to have Satan pay for this. The apostle Peter makes a statement that is fitting. He writes: "For the eyes of the Lord are over the righteous, and his ears are open unto their prayers: but the face of the Lord is against them that do evil. And who is he that will harm you if you are followers of that which is good? But and if you suffer for righteousness sake, happy are you; and be not afraid of their terror, neither be troubled" (1 Peter 3:12-14).

Even in Old Testament times, many of God's people were concerned about the problems of suffering. The prophet Habakkuk had such a burden. He struggled with the disturbing problem of God using a deplorable wicked people like the Babylonians to swallow up His people in judgment. (Hab. 1:6-13) Having seen so much wickedness and idolatry in Judah, his first question was: How God could allow His rebellious people to get away with so much sin without being punished? God answered by showing the prophet that He would soon be using the Babylonians to punish the nation of Judah. Habakkuk second question followed immediately. How could God allow a nation even more wicked and cruel than Judah to punish her? God answered by assuring the prophet that a day of reckoning would also come for the Babylonians.

The Scripture assures fellow believers that God will deal with all wickedness at the appointed time. In the meantime, ". . . the just shall live by faith" (Hab. 2:4). It is the just, for example, the righteous, who at the end will emerge victorious. The righteous must live in this world by faith in God (Romans 1:17; Gal. 3:11; Heb. 10:38), not by his own understanding. This small, prophetic and powerful book is encouraging to me. Read it to encourage yourselves.

It is often believed that suffering brings us closer to God. Webster defines "suffer" as undergoing something painful or unpleasant. James Strong, exhaustive Concordance of the Bible, defines the word "sufferings" as "pathema," meaning, to experience pain or affliction. According to Hebrew Biblical Exegesis, suffering is defined as pain or suffering that afflicts the very heart of life. It is ceaseless pain, known as affliction and suffering.

According to Theological Dictionary of the Old Testament, David E. Green says, "It is severe injury afflicting the life of the individuals, cities, or entire nations bringing them close to death. Sometimes it denotes the kind of suffering that characterizes all human existence." As we read the psalm of the cross, a prophetic psalm by King David, "My God, my God, why hast thou forsaken me? Why art thou so far from helping me, and from the words of my roaring? (Psalm 22:1). Jesus used the same words while on the cross, "MY GOD, MY GOD, WHY HAST THOU FORSAKEN ME?" (Matthew 27:46).

This is the kind of suffering Jesus encountered as He walked the Via De La Rosa to Calvary, and hung on the cross. We are told in the doctrine of election and predestination that God foreknew those who were going to be faithful to His call. For example, from the book of Romans:

> And we know that God causes all things to work together for good to those who love God, to those who are called according to his purpose. For whom He foreknew, He also predestined to become conformed to the image of His Son, that he might be the first-born among many brethren; and whom He predestined, these He also called; and who He called, these He also justified; and whom He justified, these He also glorified.

> —Romans 8: 28-30 NASB

We are also reminded in First Peter Chapter Five, "Be sober, be vigilant; because your adversary, the devil, prowls about like a lion, seeking someone to devour." "And after you have suffered for a little while, the God of all grace, who called you to His eternal glory in Christ, will Himself perfect, confirm, strengthen, and establish you" (1 Peter 5: 8, 10 NASB). These are words of assurance that despite what we are going through, God's plan for us is safe and secure.

CHAPTER 23

Summary

Something that is absolutely vital as you walk through life's journey is patience. It will help you maintain normal blood pressure, and at the same time maintain your sanity. It is not of my own ability but by the awesomeness of God, my Father, I have acquired patience. The Scriptures are replete with encouraging words that will teach you how to "Rest in the Lord with patience" (Psalm 37:7). In other words, things might look as though life is not worth living because of the obstacles that present themselves on a daily basis. Do not give up but be assured that victory is yours. Let me remind you, "No weapon that is formed against you shall prosper . . ." (Isaiah 54:17). Jesus will change your situation as you continue to be patient, and rest in Him. Get close to the Lord Jesus and constantly seek His face. Love Him with all your heart.

The Scripture says, "You shall receive power after the Holy Ghost is come upon you, and you shall be witnesses unto me both in Jerusalem, and in all Judea, and in Samaria, and unto the uttermost part of the earth" (Acts 1:8). In other words, to operate in the kingdom of God, you need the anointing, the fire of God that comes only from lingering in His presence. Get hungry for the anointing and God will surely give it to you if you remain faithful to Him. The power is in the name of Jesus. Never leave Him out of your business. He is a wonderful friend, a friend that sticks closer than a brother. He has brought me from a long way. Hell opened its doors and tried to pull me in, but Jesus stepped in and delivered me just on time to document this testimony. It's all because of Jesus I am standing in my right mind today.

Sometimes we might cry out for an easy way out, with no response. Why is God leaving me here in this situation? Let me tell you, God is not deaf, nor is He blind. So you can trust Him to bring you out of the fiery furnace with no damage to your demeanor. Whatever you are going through, as miserable as it might seem, God wants to let you know this is exactly where He wants you to be. If He does not have plans for you, life would be easy. Therefore, consider yourself blessed to be among the suffering candidates for promotion into your heavenly calling. Allow your mind to be consumed with this thought. You will have victory over the adversary in time.

Be patient. Hold on! Recognize God as your source. He has great plans for you. Your success is dependent on how you see God in your life. Do you see Him as a big God? Do you know that He is your Father and that he loves you? Then put your trust in Him and He will see you through this rough road, a road that seems eternally long with no light in view, but Jesus is the Light. He says, "I am the light of the world." (John 8:12).

Focus on that Light. Seek first His Kingdom, and always put Him first in all your undertaking. Pray about every decision you make. Obey His Word and He will give you peace. ". . . Seek peace and pursue it" (1Peter 3:11). Be willing to walk by faith and fill your mind with His Word. It can shape your thoughts. And when you get in His presence stay in that anointing. Very quietly and clearly He will speak. He says, "Be still and know that I am God . . ." (Psalm 46:10). As Jehovah Rapha, He is the God that heals. He will renew your mind if you cease to be conformed to this world.

A Final thought

To reiterate, divorce after an abusive marriage is extremely difficult for the entire family. It hurts everyone in the family, especially when children are involved. Sometimes the wounds of divorce are deep and take years to heal, emotionally and physically. Sometimes it involves death. Even when my spouse took a hammer, held it before my face without hitting me with it, but hitting the wall in front of me while I stood at the sink in the kitchen, this, to me, was a type of physical abuse. I believe what saved me was the fact that I kept quiet, not uttering a word to aggravate the situation. In view of the fact that I wanted to live, it was necessary to use wisdom. To repeat, you simply have to stay cool when you have the opportunity, and utter a prayer to the Lord in your heart. In that same vicinity my spouse held on to my blouse and twisted it at my chest, with intent to destroy my breasts saying, "Nobody else will have you!"

In his sermon recently, a pastor said, "An angry man is a dangerous man. It's a disaster waiting to happen." Why did I not think about that from the onset even though anger was obvious before the marriage? This is what happens to young people who put on blinders and refuse to admit to the obvious, hoping for a change in the behavior pattern.

Guarding the children's emotion

It is extremely difficult to be a child of divorced parents. A simple argument between parents greatly affects the emotional health of the child. Divorce destroys relationships even without having to use witchcraft. So, could you imagine forcing more destruction to the children's emotion by indulging in heavy witchcraft? It is such a pity when one's spouse indulges in witchcraft because he is so unsure of himself. He knows he is wrong, and in normal circumstances the children, having witnessed the abusive behavior will make the right choice, even though they would want to have both parents. They are forced into this position so they cannot think for themselves, because they are bound by demonic oppression willfully instilled on them by their father. What a terrible situation! He knows he is destroying the children, and the tragedy is, even those around them are affected because the devil always has his demand, and if you are his employee you are obligated to fulfill his demand. In fact, the action of the parents after divorce often disturbs the children even more than the adults. This depends on the level of maturity of the individuals. In my case the behavior of the spouse is so immature and insecure he can only turn to his evil practices.

Research shows abusive relationships happen as a result of one of the partners having experienced child abuse. Either the child was spoilt and had a habit of doing all the things he liked, or might have had an insecure childhood. You must be extremely careful about how you behave with your children while surviving divorce, after an abusive marriage. Again, it's very hard for the children since their basic security is threatened, and they want to be loyal to both parents. Therefore, if you feel you are doing a good thing by working on the children's mind you are only destroying them physically, emotionally and spiritually.

How can you balance this?

In order to maintain your sanity while surviving divorce after an abusive marriage is to forget the past and move ahead in life. Don't become angry. Instead, focus on improving your own life. Do something special for yourself. Attempt something that you wanted to do in your life but unable to because of the marriage obligations. Use your anger and frustration to make a difference for the better, and get help where and when necessary in matters you cannot handle. Take this separation as a lesson and learn from it.

Infidelity with acquaintances was taken for granted in the marriage, even during the engagement as I mentioned earlier. Although these relationships existed, I didn't see the need to use that in the divorce proceedings. In fact, I refused to make it part of the problem. The physical abuse was more than enough for a just cause.

No matter what you are going through, believe that God can remove that mountain that's hindering you. Know that it is only for a season. You are not going to die but live. Don't give up. Submitting to drugs and alcohol is not an option. Suicide is giving honor to the devil. The answer is in the Word of God. The Bible is replete with solutions for everything that's coming your way. To reiterate, Jesus Christ is the answer to every situation in your life. You cannot have His protection unless you surrender your life to Him. Through the power of the Holy Spirit, you can get to know Jesus Christ in a dynamic way. He stands with His arms open to receive you.

His invitation is, "Ho! Every one who thirsts, come to the waters; And you who have no money, come, buy and eat. Come, buy wine and milk without money and without cost. Why do you spend money for what is not bread, and your wages for what does not satisfy? Listen carefully to Me, and eat what is good, and delight yourself in abundance" (Isaiah 55: 1-2 NASB). Yes, the invitation is free. Jesus paid dearly so that we can have free access to Him. In Him there is life and peace. You have authority only as you have fellowship with Him.

The Bible tells us in John Chapter Five, there was a man in a terrible condition for 38 years. He sought healing by going to the healing pool and waiting for someone to assist him when the water was ready, to no avail. According to the Scripture, a great multitude of impotent folk were at the pool for the same reason, and took the opportunity when the occasion arose to step into the pool. This man did not have a chance. The Bible does not say how long he had been doing this, but we know from the Scripture that he had been suffering with this condition for 38 years. Nonetheless, God had been watching from the onset, and now He was ready to intervene in this man's life. Are you getting the picture? This is how God works. It's never too late for your healing and deliverance. Jesus is ready to come through for you, receive your healing right now.

Jesus is now at the scene. After questioning the impotent man, he felt such compassion for him and said, ". . . Rise, take up your bed and walk" (John 5:8). "And immediately the man was healed" (v.9). The Jews saw this as an obstacle because it was done on the Sabbath. Even in the midst of your healing ministry the religious folks would try to hinder you. Jesus was constantly being threatened by the religious authorities, but God was in control and still in control today. Even though He was threatened by the system, it did not deter Him from accomplishing His task. For example, in His call to repentance, the Scripture tells us some Pharisees came to Him and said, "Leave this place and go somewhere else. Herod wants to kill you." Jesus rebutted with a reply, "Go and tell that fox, 'Behold, I cast out demons and perform cures today and tomorrow, and the third day I reach my goal'" (Luke 13:31-32 NASB). In essence He was saying, regardless of the threat, I will openly continue to be about my Father's business. I will finish the work that I came to do.

The third day He will be perfected. He will reach His goal. He will rise triumphantly from the grave. As Jesus had compassion for the man at Bethesda in Jerusalem so he has compassion for us today. I say this with certainty because the Lord brought this Scripture to my attention two years ago. Since then I have been reading it over and over and believing God for my deliverance. Don't ever think God doesn't see what is taking place in our lives. It is because of this He was able to let me know that an enemy—Sanballat was insistent on hindering my progress. Yes, we can overcome obstacles with patience.

CHAPTER 24

Epilogue

Let me tell you, God is not deaf nor is He blind. He sees your cry and knows your trouble. If he does not have plans for you, life would be easy. So, consider yourself blessed to be among the suffering candidates for promotion into your heavenly calling. If you can allow your mind to be consumed with this thought you will make it. Be patient. Rest in the Lord. Recognize Him as your source. He has great plans for you. Your success is dependent on how you see God in your life. He is our Father and He loves us. We simply must put our trust in Him and He will see us through this rough road, a road that seems eternally long. Our Father will bring us through. He is faithful and just, and there is no one like Him.

Remember to make the Word of God part of your life. Read it daily. Never leave home without it. Pray about every decision you make. Jesus is a good example, for before He fed the multitudes, the Scripture says, "And ordering the multitudes to recline on the grass, He took the five loaves, and the two fish, and looking up toward heaven, He blessed the food; and breaking the loaves, He gave them to the disciples, and the disciples gave to the multitudes . . . And there were about five thousand men who ate, aside from women and children" (Matthew 14: 19, 21 NASB).

Note the first thing Jesus did before sharing the loaves and fish, He looked toward heaven and gave thanks. Even though He is the very God Himself, He lets us know that His priority was in communicating with the Father while He was on earth. He says, "Fear not little flock; for it is your Father's good pleasure to give you the kingdom" (Luke 12:32). He is always ready to give of His abundant love. He gave His only Son. It is Father's good pleasure to open the windows of opportunity for His children. Look to the Father and pray before every decision.

Food from the Lord

God gave me a Word today from the Prophet Isaiah Chapter Twenty Five. Here is His encouragement, not only for me, but for everyone who is reading this book. This chapter reveals a time of praise to God for the wonderful things He has done. The city of terrible nation shall fear the Lord as He defeats everyone and everything that opposes his righteous purpose and kingdom, and for His role as Deliverer and Comforter of His people. Isaiah speaks about God as one who has "been strength to the poor, strength to the needy in his distress, a refuge from the storm, and a shadow from the heat" (Isaiah 25:4). Oh, how we need His intervention.

The Scripture continues to refer to "all people" referring to the success of the proclamation of the Gospel around the world. Fat things refer to the lavish banquet, the wonderful blessings believers will experience in His presence. "He will swallow up death in victory; and the Lord God will wipe away tears from off all faces; and the rebuke of his people shall he take away from off all the earth: for the Lord has spoken it" (v.8). I have waited on the Lord with patience. In His kingdom there is no evil. No devil can over-throw His power. God is ready to destroy the veil that has been covering the eyes of His people. In fact, He has accomplished that 2000 years ago. We have to come to the realization that Jesus took care of that at Calvary when He shed His blood on the cross.

My time is in the Lord. My eyes are steadfast on Him for He is not finished with me. My holding on is not in vain. If only you can hold on, and keep your head when all around you seem to be doing well with seemingly no suffering and no persecution. You will come through victoriously. Just make sure you know Him through His Word in the Bible. I am excited about what He is doing in my life despite the fiery darts that are coming at me. I am excited for you too. He loves you with an everlasting love, a love that's unconditional and a love that will overwhelm you if only you know who you are in Him.

Remember, Jesus says, "I am in the Father, you in me and I in you" (John 14:20). Just think about that for a minute. God lets us know that we are special and that we are one with Him. If only you can get a glimpse of how He comes through for me in the middle of my mess. Jesus Christ is indeed awesome! He is the very God of the very God, lover of my soul, Rose of Sharon, Lily of the Valleys, Bright Morning Star. I love Him.

When I was beginning to feel there was no hope for recovery, Jesus picked me up and let me know it's not over. Hallelujah! It is wrong to think you are the only one going through trials. The good thing about it is that you don't have to go through alone. Jesus is walking with you. Surrender all to Him. He brought this song into my spirit a few months ago:

All to Jesus I surrender, All to Him I freely give;
I will ever love and trust Him, in His presence daily live.
I surrender all, I surrender all; All to Thee, my blessed Savior,
I surrender all.

Words: Judson W. Van DeVenter, 1855-1939
Music: Winfield S. Weeden, 1847-1908

During a discourse with His disciples about the 'Rich young ruler' who admitted that he was qualified to obtain eternal life, Jesus said:

"One thing you still lack; sell all that you possess, and distribute it to the poor, and you shall have treasure in heaven; and come, follow Me" (Luke 18:22 NASB).

The rich ruler "became very sad for he was extremely rich" (v.23).

Jesus was only testing him to see where his heart was. But he was not heavenly minded.

The apostle Peter managed to get a word in during the conversation and said, "Behold, we have left our own homes, and followed You" (v.28).

In this song, "I surrender," I asked myself, "What is it you are holding back, Mary?" Stop worrying. Let it go! We are to surrender everything to Jesus. Have no fear. Regardless of the situation He will take care of us. Trust Him and live in His presence daily.

A word from the book of Solomon, the son of King David

In the book of Solomon you can see the expression of love and the experience of love. It is known as the greatest of wedding songs written by King Solomon. He is identified as the bridegroom ("my beloved"), and his bride (my love). Apparently the book was written before Solomon had 700 wives and 300 concubines (I Kings 11:3), because he writes about monogamous marriages and the divine origin of the joy and dignity of human love in marriage. In reality, today, your first meeting is like Solomon and the Shulamite, his bride. She said, "My beloved is mine and I am his" (Solomon 2:16). There is no desire or room for any other person. In marriage there must be such a love and commitment to each other. Faithfulness to your spouse is of the utmost importance in your marriage.

As Solomon, we can say, "Hold me in your arms of grace. Please hide me in your secret place." God is your defender from life's uncertainty. Assign your wife a place of honor, a place of significance. Don't use sex as a means of taking care of an abusive encounter. This was my experience. After a physical abusive encounter, my spouse always tried to fix the problem with sex. This is insane!

Here is a declaration from Solomon Chapter Eight:

"Love is strong as death: jealousy is cruel as the grave: the coals thereof are coals of fire which hath a most vehement flame. Many waters cannot quench love, neither can the floods drown it: if a man would give all the substance of his house for love, it would utterly be con-temned" (Song of Solomon 8:6-7). In other words, it would be treated with contempt.

There is nothing more powerful and beautiful than the expression of mutual and passionate love between a bridegroom and his bride, who are fully committed to each other. But jealousy is as inflexible as the grave, a place from which no one can escape. However, a personal relationship with God will ensure confidence in a future life with Him, and the certainty that He will not abandon you to the grave. King David, the father of King Solomon, testifies about God and said, "I foresaw the Lord always before my face, for he is on my right hand, that I should not be moved. Therefore my heart rejoices, and my tongue was glad . . . also, my flesh shall rest in hope" (Acts 2:25-26). "My flesh and my heart failed: but God is the strength of my heart and my portion forever" (Psalm 73: 26).

This is absolutely encouraging to know that we are included in this proclamation. Let us all receive it and know with certainty that we are included in God's righteousness. He is exceptionally awesome and wonderful. I can attest to that.

Do you need healing in your life? Pray for someone else. Do you need a breakthrough in your situation? Pray for someone else's. Do you need God's intervention in your family affairs? Intervene for another family and God will give you peace in your situation.

Jesus breathed peace into the lives of His people. In the book of John, His words are, "Peace I leave with you, my peace I give unto you: not as the world gives . . . Let not your heart be troubled, neither let it be afraid" (John 14:27). You can encourage yourself with this Word daily.

Music ministry

The Lord had insisted that I get back to the music. I find music could be a source of healing if we apply it correctly. The Scripture talks about David using a musical instrument to bring about a healing in King Saul's life. In fact, throughout the Scriptures there are numerous documentation about music and its' effect on your spirit and mind. Hence the reason good music in the worship service on the Lord's Day is so vital. People come into the church with various issues and problems, it is amazing the difference it would make to those people who entered the service feeling downhearted, but leaving with a completely new attitude. That's how I feel when I get onto the piano at times. It revives my spirit and sets me on a new path for the day, with an entirely different attitude and zeal to move on with my chores and assignments.

Those of you who have the inclination to get involved with music through instruments or some other form, I encourage you to do so. It will become useful in the years ahead. Also, get your children involved in music. I am talking about the kind of music that encourages peace and joy. It will give them a sense of worth or belonging. Many young people are experiencing low esteem and it is showing up in their school work, and other areas of their lives.

No one detects these problems in the homes until something drastic happens or until they commit a crime. At that time you hear so many stories of how the school personnel had observed something strange about the child but did nothing about it because the system does not allow for this condition. How sad.

I have counseled people on the mission field on anger and un-forgiveness and the results were tremendous. When church families came to the altar in tears, it was not for various daily problems, but they were dealing with anger and un-forgiveness. I used my personal testimony as a means to encourage them and it was a blessing.

Despite my predicament and the terrible abuse I experienced in my marriage, I cannot remember holding any anger in my heart for any length of time. In fact, anger was not part of the territory. I was angry but didn't hold on to it. In my case there is advantage and disadvantage to this, in that in the early post-divorce days when I met my spouse during our first two daughters' wedding and marriage celebration, he was extremely charming, and pretended to be nice to me, in the presence of his second wife. Here is the disadvantage. The following week I would receive a subpoena from him to attend court, accusing me of owing him money. I don't think he is able to sleep, even though he is in another relationship. Something is terribly wrong with this picture.

Through all this, the Lord led me to a creative ability in Art—"writing and music." That kept my mind in the right direction with an attitude of gratitude. When I think that, despite the abuse, I'm still alive to be able to help others who might be going through the same treatment, and have no idea where to turn for help. Even many years after the separation, my spouse felt he had a monopoly on me. What a tragedy! He tried to maintain total control by engaging in witchcraft to hold the children hostage and to destroy me. But God is rich in mercy and continues to guide and encourage me with a song or a Word from the Bible. He does that continuously as I have fellowship with Him on a daily basis.

The fighting went on in court and out of court, and even on the streets. Fighting in the bedroom continued without saying. It was a messy situation! The attorneys were confused. They had never seen anything like that where the client is so aggressive, using a controlling spirit to control them and the court system.

Consequently, I agreed to whatever my spouse wanted. He wanted the house, that's fine by me. He wanted the money, that's fine by me. He wanted to change the accusation, I gave it up. He must not look bad on the decree. However, I have custody of the children. That didn't go too well with him, but he knew that despite the court's decision I didn't dare have those children.

I moved out after the final judgment into my new home; the woman "who is not able or won't be able to do anything for herself" is now handling herself well. Now her independence is causing him much distress. Mind you, he threatened to destroy our home if I should show any desire for it at the divorce. Now he is doing everything in his power to make sure I lose everything. It is true that I lost because of wrong decisions, but he cannot have his way forever.

However, I survived the wickedness even when I was not adept to prayer. Because of his threat my spouse has our house, yet he despised the fact that I can possess my own. So he lives on witchcraft territory. Despite his wickedness even in his senior years, I am on the Lord's side. Living alone and blessed, spouse lives with his young wife, yet unhappy.

Finally

In the face of strong opposition, you must trust God. He will give you the strength to make it. The battle is God's. Be faithful to Him. He is merciful and kind, and knows the challenges you face. Stand on God's Word, move in faith, pray with boldness and continue to work in the kingdom of God with confidence that He will reward you for your persistence and faithfulness. Take time out to thank God for what He is doing in your life. Show your appreciation and be grateful to Him for all He has done. In your pursuit of kingdom business, quitting is not an option. If you can see the invisible, you can do the impossible. If you can see it, you can have it. Close your eyes and see God in this. Remember, the Scripture says, "For I consider that the sufferings of this present time are not worthy to be compared with the glory which shall be revealed in us" (Romans 8:18).

The day comes when we will consider the trials and suffering we are facing today minute, as we begin to enter into the realm of God's glory when He shall say, "Come my child, inherit the kingdom that I have prepared for you." We can't always foresee this when trials are facing us. However, the Lord would have us to know that He has been with us all along the way, even when we couldn't see Him. Job was engulfed with questions such as "Where is God? I can't sense His presence, I am not hearing from Him."

Nonetheless, God revealed Himself to Job at the latter end. He will reveal His glory to us in due time. There is no searching of His understanding. He does not become weary or tired. "He gives strength to the weary, and to him who lacks might He increases power. Though youth grow weary and tired, and vigorous young men stumble badly, yet those who wait for the LORD will gain new strength; they will mount up with wings like eagles. They will run and not get tired. They will walk and not faint" (Isaiah 40: 29-31 NASB).

Because of Christ's Resurrection we can walk in the power of the Holy Spirit and experience miracles and blessings in our lives. So don't give up because God has not given up on the dreams He put in your heart. If He can push me along to make my dreams materialize, He certainly can do the same for you. I challenge you to push your way with a made-up mind and ask God to show you what he wants to accomplish through you, or in your life. You are unique and you can declare, as King David, "I am fearfully and wonderfully made" (Psalm 139:14). Rest assured God has something important for you to do. He will give you the dream for your life if you trust Him. He wants to fulfill His sovereign purposes for you. Instead of worrying, rest in His love.

Compassion mixed with faith

Let me give you an idea of what I mean when I talk about compassion mixed with faith. On one of my trips to Grenada, my sister requested that I bring some alive or other pain medication for her maid's father who was dying of cancer. When I arrived home my sister was away for a week, but the young woman who worked for her was ready to leave because there was little hope of getting home unless someone stopped and gave her a ride on this holiday season. On the Island, businesses were closed during the holidays, including bus services. So she looked forward to getting some means of transportation to take her home. I gave her the tablets for her father and decided to travel with her.

I said to her, "I want to pray with your father." Her response was, "even if we get a ride from here, how are you going to get back?"

"Don't worry about it. God will make a way for me." I replied.

She completed her day's work, and we left, hoping to get a ride to her home. The road was mountainous, a long distance and many miles from my sister's home. We definitely could not walk that distance. One thing about the Island, a driver coming from or going to the country would willingly stop to give you a ride. With that in mind, my hope was high, providing someone is traveling in that direction.

At last we got a ride going, and the driver was kind enough to leave us on the main road leading to the young woman's home where her father was laying ill in bed. Now we have to climb a steep hill to get to the house where she and her parents reside. We walked up that long stretch. Walking up slowly, we arrived at her place. She is used to that stretch, but for me it was quite a journey, resulting in much pain at the back of my legs after stretching them to the limit. We arrived at her home. Her parents lived next door. I found her father emaciated and flat in bed wearing pampers. He communicated well, verbally. I ministered to him from the Scriptures, specifically from James Chapter Five, washed and anointed him, and said a short prayer. The Scripture reads:

> Is any among you suffering? Let him pray. Is anyone cheerful? Let him sing praises. Is anyone among you sick? Let him call for the elders of the church; and let them pray over him, anointing him with oil in the name of the Lord; and the prayer offered in faith will restore the one who is sick, and the Lord will raise him up, and if he has committed sins, they will be forgiven him.
>
> —James 5: 13-15 NASB

Please note, ". . . The prayer of faith shall save the sick, and the Lord shall raise him up . . ." (James 5:15). The key here is 'faith.' All through the New Testament, it was faith that caused Jesus to respond to the need of the people in a positive way. I share about the many instances where Jesus brought healing to many individuals because of their faith, or the faith of their friends. So before leaving this 77 year-old man's bedside, assisted by his wife and daughter I tried moving him, to no avail. So I left, hoping he would feel better even though he was experiencing much pain. He was a Methodist, but his daughter had her church family pray with him once during his illness.

I left the home, and his daughter began to walk down that hill with me. I told her, it made no sense coming with me, having to walk up that hill again, it's much too tiring. She insisted, "How are you going to get home? I want to make sure you get a ride." She said.

"Don't worry about it, I'll get home." I replied.

She insisted on taking me part of the way and I encouraged her to return home because I was confident the Lord had a 'Good Samaritan' on the road. She surrendered and returned home.

For you to understand this trip you really have to have an idea of the countryside of the Island. Apart from 'being the land of spice,' Grenada is known for its' hills and mountains. Not just a simple hill but I am talking about those steep hills where you have to stop and breathe as you walk. During a work day the bus travels along those roads. Nonetheless, the natives are well acquainted with those types of hills and seem to be able to handle them well. So, I simply wanted to prove that God is who He says He is. The Scripture says, "And without faith it is impossible to please Him, for he who comes to God must believe that He is, and that He is a rewarder to those who seek him" (Hebrews 11:6 NASB).

I proved God as an empty bus seemed to be going my way. I stopped the driver and he agreed to take me home. So here was God at work because of perseverance and compassion despite the transportation problem, and the mountainous area in which I had to climb. He gave me the strength and showed mercy.

The next day, the patient's daughter called me from her second job in the City to say her mother called her to report that her father got out of bed last night and was heard walking in the dark, in the kitchen, completely healed. What a miracle. Praise God. The Lord did a great work. When I returned to America, I followed up on his condition and was told that he was back in the garden doing his business as usual, even climbing mango trees, and assisting his daughter with business transactions in the city.

I just wanted to share God's miraculous intervention on the mission field. In this case, faith had much to do with it, moving up the mountain not knowing how I was getting back home. But God proved His faithfulness to me.

In those days I didn't have to work up a faith, but the faith that was already instilled in me without my knowing, was put to work automatically. Today, because the problems and cares of this world are so overwhelming, faith seems to dwindle, and one tends to forget that "Jesus Christ is the same yesterday and today and forever"(Hebrews 13:8). I had to get back on tract and put my trust in Him. As I think about putting faith to work, a good example comes to mind: In the Gospel of Mark Chapter Two we are told that four men took their sick friend on his bed to see Jesus. The Scripture says that Jesus had come back to Capernaum, and the news went abroad that He was at home. The crowd gathered together so that there was no room even at the door. While Jesus was speaking to them, the Scripture says, "they brought unto Him a paralytic, carried by four men." Unable to get to Him on account of the crowd, they removed the roof above Him and when they had made an opening, they let down the pallet/bed on which the paralytic was lying" (Mark 2:1-4). When Jesus saw their faith, he said unto the paralytic, "Son, your sins are forgiven" (Mark 2: 5).

It is clear that Jesus healed the sick as a result of his friends' faith. Therefore, it's a good thing to hang around positive people, so that in the event things happen in your life you can call on people of faith to agree with you for deliverance. Sometimes all you need is faith and belief in God. Faith was seen not in the patient but in his friends. "When Jesus saw their faith." It was his friends' faith that caused Jesus to respond to the sick by saying "Son, your sins are forgiven." For the same reason, it behooves us to have compassion for lost souls and bring them to Jesus. We need to pray that every nation will come to know Jesus as Lord. They need to know that He is their only hope of salvation.

The man in Grenada was extremely ill with no hope of recovery as far as the natural mind. In fact, I looked at him in bed and assumed I was there to perform the last rites. Then I thought coming this way could not be in vain, because I came expecting a miracle. Before I entered his home I had no idea what his condition was, but I was told he was dying of cancer. Nonetheless, I was in the Island and I like to pray. As a result, God was likely to do something spectacular for the man. God declared in the book of Jeremiah, "I am the Lord, the God of all flesh, is there anything too hard for me?" (Jeremiah 32:27). On my missionary journeys I took God's Word seriously and put it to work. My experience tells me, if you work the Word it will work for you. With no transportation, and no imminent transport to take me back home, I moved in faith believing that the Lord would not leave me at the roadside in distress.

When you are determined, your friends must see Jesus in you regardless of whose roof gets broken into. Those four men in Jesus' day were determined to help their friend. The roof can be taken care of later. Are you afraid of moving out in faith today? Moses in the Old Testament time was commissioned and he said, "I am not eloquent, I am slow of speech and of a slow tongue." God's reply to him was, "Who has made man's mouth?" (Exodus 4:10-11).

If we take these things into consideration, we ought to know that there is nothing impossible with God. The same work He did in yonder days, it is the same work He is doing today. Put your faith and trust in Him. Your faith will keep the enemy at bay. With the shield of faith, you can ward off the fiery darts of the enemy who comes to try you. Remember the Scripture, "Without faith it is impossible to please God."

The woman who had an issue of blood for twelve years had seen many physicians yet was no better. In fact, the Scripture says her condition grew worse. When she heard of Jesus she pressed in with the intent to touch His garment. "For she said if I may but touch his clothes I shall be whole. By this simple faith, Jesus felt virtue left Him. He turned and asked, "Who touched me?"

When He saw the woman and perceived what she had done, He said to her, "Daughter, your faith has made you whole; go in peace, and be whole of your plague" (Mark 5:25-34).

Yes, like this woman, let us consider her statement; "If I may but touch his clothes." That simple faith will do it. Let us encourage ourselves with this kind of faith that we may be free from bondage and fear. This miracle is intended for you and for me. Let us touch Jesus. As we read the Word, receive it, meditate on it, and touch Him in the Spirit. In the name of Jesus Christ, Hallelujah! You don't have to nurse your problems and keep it all to yourself, give it to Jesus. Simply touch Him in faith. In other words, believe that He can release you of your burdens now. Get in His presence in worship. He loves you with an everlasting love, and He has created you for worship. When you worship He has no choice but to lavish on you His special favor. All you have to do is ask. You have not, because you asked not. "Ask and it shall be given you; seek, and you shall find; knock, and it shall be opened unto you" (Mathew 7: 7).

In essence this is my life

Inclusive is childhood parental abuse, attempted rape as a child, abusive marriage both physically and emotionally. Nonetheless, this opened the door to higher education. In other words, I insisted not to have a pity party, but to endeavor a better life academically and spiritually. Even while I was employed as a professional nurse in administration, extracurricular activities in the realm of academia and theological studies kept my mind occupied, despite the evil that was set up to destroy me. The Scripture says, "God is faithful, who will not suffer you to be tempted above that you are able; but will with the temptation also make a way to escape, that you may be able to bear it" (1 Corinthians 10:13). With this promise, we are able to persevere despite the persecution.

Today, as a retired nurse I enjoy some of what God expects of me: "writing, music, and inter-ceding" for His people. The obstacles are horrendous but I am not giving up because it is certain God will see me through.

It's a dangerous thing to live in the same home during the divorce proceedings, especially when the divorce is contested by the abuser. I was not going to leave the home and he had no intention of leaving, as his plan was to keep the children despite the court's decision to let me have custody of them.

Divorce became final on November 1972.

Reason: "Cruel and inhuman treatment."

As per the divorce decree, "Defendant moved in open court with the consent of plaintiff to amend his answer to include a cause of action for divorce on the grounds of cruelty, the plaintiff having withdrawn her complaint and the defendant having proceeded on his cause of action for cruelty and testimony having been taken in open court in support of the allegations of the cause of action for cruelty, satisfactorily proving said cause of action. The defendant hereby granted judgment dissolving the marriage relation existing between Mary—plaintiff and George—defendant, by reason of the cruelty to defendant caused by plaintiff . . ." and so on. Are you getting the picture here? You might ask, "Why have you given up your rights?" Had I known that after all these years the demons would still be at work, I would hold out for my right and for the truth, but there is more to life than these trivialities. Despite his getting his attorney to have him look good on court documents, he is still unable to have peace. As a result, I must not live in peace.

Deeding all rights

Deeding all my rights, title and interest in property to defendant . . . "The plaintiff—shall have custody of the four infant children, with visitation rights to defendant." He didn't object to that because he knew of his plan to keep the children by force. (1). He refused to abide by the court's order. (2). I am limited to where I can go with the children, not more than 50 miles from Times Square, New York. (3). Child support of $45. a week for 4 children. (4). Plaintiff waves any and all rights to support or alimony for herself. (5). He insisted, ordered and decreed and plaintiff agrees that the children are never to be left solely in the care of plaintiff's mother at any time during their infancy. (6). Plaintiff will immediately obtain daytime employment during the normal daytime hours. Do you see the audacity in the demands that he makes in court? Do you see the insanity? Can you get a picture of the life I have been living? He dictates how I ought to live even after I am separated from him.

Those were his demands and the court must go along with his requests. Again, can you get the picture of the demonic activity taking place here? The attorneys are being controlled, and the children are being controlled and brainwashed by witchcraft.

Despite his control of the Court's system and the attorneys, my spouse is yet not satisfied, and continued his harassment by stalking me and refusing to hand over the children. In an attempt to make my life miserable, he is making the children part of his product by handing them over to the devil, not being able to use the free will God has given them. However, God is my defense. He sees and knows, and will judge accordingly.

I am the abuser, yet he is stalking me. I am the abuser yet he is asking me to enter into matrimony with him a second time. He became so angry and vowed I will never have peace. But peace is not his to give. According to John 14:27, Jesus is the

Author of peace. God is awesome. He is my Father. He is Jehovah Nissi—His banner over us is love.

Today, regardless of what you go through, do not be overwhelmed by the trials and persecution that want to overtake you. Trust God. He promises to deliver you in every trial. He is the same God that delivered Daniel and his friends from the lion's den and the fiery furnace. He will deliver you, too. Have good counsel before entering the doctrine of matrimony. Godly counseling is preferable. Be willing to heed good advice. Know that counseling is ordained of God when it is not based on feeling, but on the solid Word of God. You will feel a witness deep down in your soul. One might call it a gut feeling. Put your partner to the test over tea or music. Spend time in fellowship over lunch and get a sense of where he is, as opposed to where you are. Once you have taken that step, work at it. Engage yourself in something that is appealing to you. Get involved in community work or occupy yourself in what God has called you to be. Don't murmur or complain. Do everything onto the honor and glory of God. Get involved in worship and find a Bible-believing church where you can grow in Christ, and in the knowledge of God, then stay in His anointing. The Word of God says, "Let us draw near with a true heart in sincerity, in full assurance of faith and having our hearts sprinkled from evil conscience with humility" (Hebrews 10:22). Enrich your mind with the Word of God. The Scripture says, "Be not conformed to this world, but be transformed by the renewing of your mind . . ." (Romans 12: 2a). Transform your mind by indulging in the truth, so that you can know the will of God for your life. We have to get to the point of accepting our circumstances and be free of bitterness. It is not going to be easy. You have to let go and devote yourself to worship regardless of what is happening or has happened in your life. As you are privileged to know God of all grace, be generous in your praise and thanksgiving on a daily basis.

Nehemiah was in a challenging situation. He was the king's cupbearer who had a huge burden. He needed favor and success from the king to start the work in Jerusalem. For days he mourned and fasted and prayed. He did not know what would happen, or that one day God would call on him to rebuild the walls of Jerusalem. Nehemiah just knew that he was overwhelmed with burdens. As servants of God we are sometimes faced with tremendous burdens for our people, especially if we are intercessors and praying people. Nehemiah was such a person. He was God's praying servant and knew that he could not succeed without Him. His people needed a miracle from God, and because he cried out to Him, God granted him favor. As we go through life, no matter what our situation or our resources, we need to realize that our lives are in God's hands. We can call on Him for help with our marriages, our children, our families, financial miracle, and relationships. Like Nehemiah and the other Old Testament saints, remember that you can depend on God. Know that He is ready to hear you and provide what you need.

In your life, remember to stay humble before God. Trust in God and His Word. His promise is true. Ask Him for wisdom and understanding. Recognize that you owe everything to God. Glorify Him and don't cease to praise Him, in Jesus' name. Don't let fear rule your life as "God has not given us a spirit of fear, but of power, and of love and of a sound mind" (2 Timothy 1:7).

Commit your life to living according to Biblical principles and to being pure and holy in God's sight. Follow Jesus and resist the influences of the world. Seek to stay vigilant and clean before God. Strive to be free from compromise and anything that pollutes your mind and heart. In your life, you may experience delays, uncertainties and problems. You may not see God's promises being fulfilled in the way in which you anticipated. Your prayers may not seem to be answered. You may not see tangible results from your work. But always remember that the essence of our Christian life is to continue to serve and believe and have faith in God no matter what happens. Remember you are clay and God still is the potter. No matter how old you are, and what you have done, He still has the right to point you in a new direction, shape you in a new way. Don't fight God, and don't resist His leading. Instead, seek to stay before Him always submitting your life to Him. Be sensitive to the leading of His Spirit. Let Him shape you, and, if He pleases, reshape you. The same God who delivered the children of Israel from Egypt is by your side. He can deliver you from any trial. He can perform miracles to meet your needs. He can solve problems that don't seem to have solutions.

As God's children, we are beneficiaries of His grace and favor. This means, He pours out His abundance on us. He opens doors when they seem shut. He gives victory when defeat seems inevitable. He gives wisdom that no human mind could comprehend. The Scripture says, "Seek the LORD while he may be found, call upon him while he is near" (Isaiah 55:6). The Scripture also says, "Let us draw near with a true heart . . ." (Hebrews 10:22). Grow more intimate in this relationship. Feast on His Word, and look for His favor in every situation. Continually live in full expectation that He is with you.

I pray that this book will enlighten and bless you in many areas of your lives. Most of all that you will invite the Lord Jesus as your partner and friend in all you do and say. He is awesome and is willing to embrace you in time of distress. He will heal your broken heart and give you peace if you put Him first in your undertaking. Without Him I would not be alive to share my testimony with you today. Do not leave Him out of your business. I used my post-abusive marriage and divorce to further my education and keep myself busy by helping others on the mission field and at home. As Jesus had compassion for the sick we, too, ought to have compassion for the unsaved and for those who are left without Jesus. Talking from experience, having compassion for the sick will bring immediate healing for the individual. In the New Testament, those who sought Jesus for healing for their loved ones did so because they had compassion; and in order to have a vibrant and viable ministry one must have compassion for the lowly for they are all God's people. Hallelujah!

Near the Cross

❉

Jesus, keep me near the cross, There a precious fountain
Free for all, a healing stream, Flows from Calvary's mountain

Near the cross, a trembling soul, Love and mercy found me,
There the Bright and Morning Star Sheds its beams around me

Near the cross! O Lamb of God, Bring its scenes before me;
Help me walk from day to day With its shadows o'er me.

Near the cross I'll watch and wait, Hoping, trusting ever,
Till I reach the golden strand Just beyond the river

Refrain

In the cross, in the cross
Be my glory ever;
Till my raptured soul shall find
Rest beyond the river

Fanny J. Crosby
William H. Doane

Notes

All Scriptures were taken from the King James (KJV)
Version of the Bible, New American Standard Bible (NASB),
King James Amplified Version (AMP),

Author's Biography

A small Island in the Caribbean, where the soil is rich in minerals, and known as the land of spice, Dr. Mary Johnson was born on that soil, the Island of Grenada. The first of seven children, she was the recipient of harsh punishment from her mother, and the victim of attempted rape twice as a child. She migrated to Aruba with her siblings to join her parents where she completed most of her academic education. The spoken language was Dutch, a new experience but learning a new language was a good thing. Dr. Johnson received her nursing education and post graduate midwifery in London, England. Met and married George Preudhomme in London, Dr. Johnson worked as a practicing midwife after graduation. At the invitation of her sister, she migrated to America with her family to work in medicine.

Dr. Johnson is a retired nurse and missionary to the nations, author of the book "Branded for Missions" published by Author House in 2005. She is the recipient of a Bachelor's Degree in Sociology, Bachelor's Degree in Religious Education, Master's Degree in Health Care Administration, Master's Degree in Theology, and a Doctorate Degree in Theology, Ph.D. Missionary of 20 years, she ministered in New York City, the Caribbean Islands, including Grenada, Trinidad and Tobago, St. Vincent and the Grenadines, Jamaica, and lastly, Bolivia—South America. She travelled extensively throughout the nations including England, India, China, Asia, the Philippines, Hong Kong, Israel, Rome, Egypt, and Bolivia—South America. She relocated to Florida to escape the many years of bitter cold weather, not without challenges. Her spouse vowed she'll never be happy with another man; but God is faithful to see her through. She enjoys playing the piano as the Lord insists that she continue her music.